DEFENDING FREE SPEECH

Selected Commentary by the Ayn Rand Institute

EDITED AND WITH
AN INTRODUCTION
AND ESSAYS BY

STEVE SIMPSON

Director of Legal Studies, The Ayn Rand Institute

ADDITIONAL ESSAYS BY
ONKAR GHATE, ELAN JOURNO AND LEONARD PEIKOFF

AYN RAND
INSTITUTE PRESS

First Printing 2016

Religious Terrorism vs. Free Speech
© 1989 Leonard Peikoff. Used by permission

Other articles in this volume reprinted by permission from
the original publisher.

ISBN: 978-0-9794661-8-2

AynRand.org

CONTENTS

INTRODUCTION: A BATTLE OF IDEAS

Civilization depends on reason; freedom means the freedom to think, then act accordingly; the rights of free speech and a free press implement the sovereignty of reason over brute force. If civilized existence is to be possible, the right of the individual to exercise his rational faculty must be inviolable.

—Leonard Peikoff, 1989

Freedom of speech is an essential pillar of Western civilization, yet, tragically, this precious right has come under increasing attack over the last few decades—in the fatwah against Salman Rushdie in 1989, the threats against Danish cartoonists in 2005-06, and, more recently, the attacks on *Charlie Hebdo* in Paris and on a cartoon contest in Garland, Texas. While the chief perpetrators of the attacks have been Islamic totalitarians, the primary threat to freedom of speech is not existential, but philosophical. Islamists are obviously motivated by ideas that are anathema to freedom of speech, but so, increasingly, are Western leaders and intellectuals, who have repeatedly met these attacks not with a confident defense of Western values, but with apologies, appeasement, and victim-blaming.

For a glimpse of the source of these ideas, we need look no further than the universities, where students are taught a steady diet of irrationalism and emotionalism, self-sacrifice, and multicultural tribalism. The results are predictable—students increasingly seek "trigger warnings" before being taught controversial ideas, they seek refuge in "safe spaces," and they rail against the ideals on which Western culture is based. In 2015 we saw the logical consequences of these ideas, when students at the University of Missouri physically blocked a photographer from taking pictures of a protest held on public property, and one professor was caught on camera calling for "some muscle" to remove a student who refused to stop filming the protests.

Meanwhile, our politicians increasingly use the "muscle" they possess—the power of physical force, which is the essence of government power—to threaten free speech directly and to choke it off through the use of regulation and litigation. Recent examples include the IRS's targeting of Tea Party groups for attempting to speak out during the 2012 election cycle, the constant calls by politicians and intellectuals for greater controls on political speech in the form of campaign finance laws, demands that the United States enact European-style "hate speech" laws, and the investigations by state attorneys general of Exxon and various advocacy groups for challenging climate change orthodoxy.

Ayn Rand spent much of her career writing about events such as these and the philosophical ideas and trends that produce them. In her article "Choose Your Issues," which appeared in the first issue of the *Objectivist Newsletter*, she wrote: "[T]wo enormously dangerous issues are creeping up on us, undiscussed, unopposed and unfought. . . one to destroy intellectual freedom, the other to destroy economic freedom." The first was censorship; the second was rampant business regulation, most notably the antitrust laws. Rand urged her readers to educate themselves and speak out about these issues as "they involve the fundamental principles of our culture." In her 1960 essay "For the New Intellectual," she elaborated on this point: "*Intellectual* freedom cannot exist without *political* freedom; political freedom cannot exist without *economic* freedom; *a free mind and a free market are corollaries.*"

At the Ayn Rand Institute, we have carried on the defense of both intellectual and economic freedom that Rand began over fifty years ago. The current volume is a collection of our recent writings, published on our website and as op-eds, on the subject of free speech. With one exception, all the pieces have been published since 2003. The exception, which serves as a prologue to the essays in Part 1 of the book, is Leonard Peikoff's article on our government's shameful response to the fatwah against Salman Rushdie. In 2009, two decades after the incident, the writer Bruce Bawer would note in his book, *Surrender*, that "there were precious few of us who grasped at the time of the Rushdie fatwah that here was indeed a new form of jihad on the world scene" and that Islamists presented a grave threat to intellectual freedom.

Peikoff grasped it in 1989, shortly after Iran's Ayatollah Khomeini issued the fatwah and Western governments did nothing.

His piece, which ran in the *New York Times* as a full-page advertisement, is a philosophical tour de force, a grave warning of what will happen if we do not act, and a call to action in defense of our rights.

Peikoff identifies the fatwah for what it is—an act of war—a term that even today most commentators are loath to use. Decrying the lame and equivocal response by our government to the Ayatollah's declaration of war, Peikoff explains just what our government was sacrificing: the values of reason and intellectual freedom that are at the heart of Western civilization. The consequences of inaction, as Peikoff explained, were dire:

> If [the Ayatollah] is not stopped . . . writers and publishers will begin, as a desperate measure of self-defense, to practice self-censorship . . . . Is the land of the free and the home of the brave to become the land of the bland and the home of the fearful?

Tragically, the events of the last decade have proved Peikoff correct. Our leaders and intellectuals have continued to appease the enemies of Western civilization and the consequences are now clear: increased attacks, widespread fear and self-censorship, and a growing antipathy to free speech in the West.

But while some commentators have noted these consequences, none has focused on the fundamental philosophical causes of the attacks and of the weak response among intellectuals and governments in the West.

As this volume attests, at ARI we engage in this sort of analysis every day.

Along with Peikoff's essay, the essays in Part 1 of this book serve as a demonstration of the principle that ideas have consequences, and terrible ideas have terrible consequences. The essays in this part expand on the points raised in Peikoff's essay, discussing the major terrorist attacks on free speech that followed the Rushdie affair, the ideas and attitudes that motivated both the attacks and the appeasing response in the West, and the self-censorship that has taken root in the West as a result. This section also includes my essay on North Korea's threats to Sony over the movie *The Interview*, because the episode closely parallels the blame many unjustly placed on private companies for the inactions of their governments during the Rushdie affair. In addition to essays, Part 1 includes an interview of Flemming Rose, the Danish editor at the center of the Muhammad cartoons controversy in 2005 and author of *The Tyranny of Silence: How One Cartoon Ignited a Global Debate on the Future of Free Speech*. Part 1 ends with a timeline of significant events related to terrorist attacks on free speech since the Rushdie affair, illustrating what the West's appeasement has wrought.

Parts 2 and 3 examine the ideas motivating the attacks on freedom of speech more broadly, their consequences, and what we need to do to defend this precious right.

What are the ideas at the root of the attacks on free speech? In

1962 Ayn Rand summarized them as "mysticism (irrationalism)—altruism—collectivism." These ideas threaten more than just freedom of speech, as Rand made clear; they are eroding the foundations of Western civilization itself.

Irrationalism, whether secular or religious, represents a rejection of our basic means of survival—our reasoning minds. In her essay "Faith and Force: The Destroyers of the Modern World," Rand noted the consequences of rejecting reason: "There are only two means by which men can deal with one another: guns or logic. Force or persuasion. Those who know that they cannot win by means of logic, have always resorted to guns." The entire jihadist attack on free speech serves as a grim reminder that Rand was right. In my essay "At the Heart of the Attacks on Speech, an Attack on Reason," I examine the role of mysticism and irrationalism in the context of both the Islamist attacks on speech and the ideas motivating the rejection of free speech on America's campuses.

Altruism is captured in the popular dictum that we are "our brother's keeper." It is the doctrine that individuals have no right to exist for their own sakes or to pursue their own happiness as they see fit, but must instead put the interests of others before their own. In *Atlas Shrugged*, Rand made the point (speaking through John Galt) that "Those who start by saying: 'It is selfish to pursue your own wishes, you must sacrifice them to the wishes of others'—end up by saying: 'It is selfish to uphold your own convictions, you must sacrifice them to the convictions of others.'" In "The Twilight of Freedom of Speech," Onkar Ghate illustrates how this principle is causing the West to sacrifice its convictions—including the conviction that freedom of speech is essential—to the Islamists.

Collectivism follows naturally from mysticism and altruism. It holds that the individual has no real existence or value apart from the group, and that his primary concern should be to devote himself to the "common good." Collectivism, as Rand put it in "Who Will Protect Us from Our Protectors," views "man as a congenital incompetent, a helpless, mindless creature who must be fooled and ruled by a special elite with some unspecified claim to superior wisdom and a lust for power." Thus, Islamists command us to obey the dictates of all-powerful imams, and secular collectivists in America claim that the "collective rights" of the "public" trump the right of the individual to think and say what he wants. I examine one of the most pernicious examples of this latter view in Part 3, which addresses campaign finance laws and the contemporary attack on political speech.

There are many more essays in this volume than those mentioned here, each dealing with various aspects of the attacks on free speech and, importantly, the principles—reason, egoism, and individual rights—that are necessary to defend it. Those familiar with ARI's work will know that we produce philosophical and cultural commentary in many forms, including not only writings, but courses, talks, and videos as well. For those interested in learning more about how Rand's ideas apply to the issues covered in this volume, we include a list of further resources at the end.

Ayn Rand saw herself as resurrecting in philosophically stronger form the ideas of the Enlightenment and, in particular, defending the ideas and values on which America, her adopted homeland, was founded. While Rand harshly criticized those who attacked these foundations, her ultimate focus was always on the positive—the ideas and values on which a proper human life should be based. This volume is compiled in the same spirit, and we think you will see that the approach we take at ARI is never simply to criticize bad ideas and trends, but to promote better ones in their place.

Steve Simpson
Irvine, California
April 2016

PART 1

The War on Free Speech

The truly and deliberately evil men are a very small minority; it is the appeaser who unleashes them on mankind; it is the appeaser's intellectual abdication that invites them to take over. When a culture's dominant trend is geared to irrationality, the thugs win over the appeasers. When intellectual leaders fail to foster the best in the mixed, unformed, vacillating character of people at large, the thugs are sure to bring out the worst. When the ablest men turn into cowards, the average men turn into brutes.

—Ayn Rand, "Altruism as Appeasement,"
The Objectivist

The Rushdie Affair: Prelude to 9/11

Religious Terrorism
vs. Free Speech

Leonard Peikoff March 21, 1989

Ayatollah Khomeini's attack on Salman Rushdie and his publishers represents religious terrorism. Americans oppose the Ayatollah's death-decree, but our government is doing nothing to combat it.

President George H. W. Bush has issued a limp condemnation coupled with the vague statement that Iran would be held "accountable" if American interests are harmed. But two California bookstores have already been bombed, a New York weekly newspaper has been demolished by firebombing, at least 178 threats of death or destruction have been received by booksellers nationwide, major American publishers (primarily Viking) are barricaded at ruinous cost behind an army of private security guards—and every American author, speaker, and reader must wonder if and when he will become a target of armed Islamic fundamentalists with orders to kill heretics.

Has Bush become the new Jimmy Carter? Carter wrung his hands and did nothing while Iran held Americans hostage. This time Iran is attempting to hold our minds hostage.

A religious motive does not excuse murder; it makes the crime more dangerous. It took the West centuries to move from medieval mysticism to the Enlightenment, and thereby discover the only safeguard against endless, bloody, religious warfare: the recognition of man's inalienable right to think and speak as he chooses. Civilization depends on reason; freedom means the freedom to think, then act accordingly; the rights of free speech and a free press implement the sovereignty of reason over brute force. If civilized existence is to be possible, the right of the individual to exercise his rational faculty must be inviolable.

This article originally appeared as an advertisement in the *New York Times* in 1989.

The ultimate target of the Ayatollah, as of all mystics, is not a particular "blasphemy," but reason itself, along with its cultural and political expressions: science, the Industrial Revolution, the American Revolution. If the assault succeeds, the result will be an Age of Unreason—a new Dark Ages. As Ayn Rand wrote in *Philosophy: Who Needs It*, in her prescient 1960 essay "Faith and Force: The Destroyers of the Modern World":

> The conflict of reason versus mysticism is the issue of life or death—or freedom or slavery—or progress or stagnant brutality. . . . Reason is the only objective means of communication and of understanding among men; when men deal with one another by means of reason, reality is their objective standard and frame of reference. But when men claim to possess supernatural means of knowledge, no persuasion, communication or understanding is possible.

Many people have denounced the Ayatollah's threats, but have then undercut their own stand by offering apologies to those whose "sensibilities" the book has "offended." No apology is necessary. No creed, Islamic or otherwise, which leads to "holy terror" can demand respect from civilized men.

Whether Rushdie's book in particular is good or evil, noble or depraved, is now irrelevant. Once death is threatened, there is only one issue to discuss and defend: an individual's right to speak, whether anyone or everyone likes what he says or not. "Blasphemy" violates no one's rights. Those who feel insulted do not have to listen to or read the insults. In defending religious liberty, Jefferson observed that "the operations of the mind" must not be made "subject to the coercion of the laws," adding:

> The legitimate powers of government extend to such acts only as are injurious to others. But it does me no injury for my neighbor to say there are twenty gods, or no God. It neither picks my pocket nor breaks my leg.

If blasphemy is the issue, we submit that a religious dictator inciting murder is blasphemy against the sanctity of human life. It is said that Rushdie's book impugns the faith of believers. So does science. It is said that the book is offensive to the values of the Ayatollah's followers. So is the United States of America.

Why has the outrage felt by the American public not been translated into a call for action against Iran? The protests from both the Right and the Left in this country ring hollow because both groups have betrayed the philosophic ideas necessary to act.

Conservatives have become dominated by religionists, who openly base their views on mystical dogma and want the government to impose their dogmas by force which is just what the Ayatollah is doing. Homegrown fundamentalists are in no position to lead a crusade for free thought. Can these groups maintain that it is wrong to ban Rushdie, but right to ban Darwin?

All of us owe a debt of gratitude to liberal groups like PEN and the Author's Guild for their courageous condemnation of the Ayatollah's threats. But these groups do not offer principled opposition, either—because of their philosophic commitment to collectivism and cultural relativism. Liberals characteristically hold that individual rights must be sacrificed to the "public good," and that Western civilization is no better than the "culture" of tribal savages. Those who counsel appeasement as a principle of foreign policy will not and cannot demand action against the Ayatollah.

The response of many commentators has been to place the blame, incredibly, on American businessmen: in particular, on the booksellers, such as Waldenbooks, who are damned for trying to protect the safety of their employees and customers. It is not the responsibility of private citizens to risk their lives in defying a foreign power when our government, whose duty it is to protect our lives, turns a blind eye on an historic crime.

Terrorism unpunished is terrorism emboldened. The Ayatollah has already broadened his attacks; he is now threatening death to anyone who criticizes Islam. If he is not stopped, who can predict where the next threat to our publishers and bookstores will come from? From Palestinian terrorists offended by a pro-Israeli book? From the kind of anti-abortion or animal-rights groups that now bomb clinics or trash research laboratories? Do we want a country in which people are afraid to walk into bookstores, because raids on such stores have become an uncontested form of protest?

The clear and present danger is that writers and publishers will begin, as a desperate measure of self-defense, to practice self-censorship—to speak, write, and publish with the implicit thought in mind: "What group will this offend and to what acts of aggression will I then be vulnerable?" The result would be the death of the First

Amendment and the gradual Finlandization of America. Is the land of the free and the home of the brave to become the land of the bland and the home of the fearful?

In contrast to both the religious right and the relativist left, [we] uphold the necessity for government action in the present crisis—government action to protect the rights of Americans to their lives, safety, and freedom. A nation that allows the agents of a foreign power to terrorize its citizens with impunity on their own soil has lost the will to survive.

We call for three specific actions:

(1) Police and other government security protection must be given on request to any publisher, bookstore, or other victim who has received a demonstrable threat in connection with the Rushdie affair. It is a monstrous injustice for such victims to be bled dry by security costs while the government neglects its proper duty.

(2) In light of the Ayatollah's decree and the record of his followers, their incitement to murder constitutes a criminal act, which must be punished. If the inciters are foreign nationals, they should be deported.

(3) The United States government (alone or with allies) should take military action against Iran, until the Iranian government rescinds the Ayatollah's death decree. The Ayatollah's threat against American lives is an act of war. It calls for reprisals. Targets should include the known training camps where Iranian terrorists are being schooled and bred.

Force used in self-defense, retaliatory force striking back at those who initiate violence, is a moral necessity. To adopt a pacifist stance—or to engage in infinite behind-the-scenes "negotiations" that lead nowhere—is to surrender the world to brutality. Timid half-measures are worse than none; one does not respond to murder merely by withdrawing ambassadors or cutting back on trade. One cannot appeal to reason in dealing with those who reject it. Force is the only language intelligible to those who live by force.

The only life the Ayatollah has a right to declare forfeit is his own.

The Danish Cartoons Crisis: A Weaker West

Free Speech in the Balance

Christian Beenfeldt and *Onkar Ghate*   February 10, 2006

A battle for Western freedom is being fought overseas. The specific object of the battle is merely a handful of cartoons. The outcome of the struggle, however, will reverberate for years.

The conflict began when the leading Danish newspaper, *Jyllands-Posten*, printed twelve cartoons of Muhammad to expose and challenge the country's existing climate of fear of criticizing Islam. Confirming the newspaper's nightmares, the response was the deluge of Islamic rage, death threats and violence now sweeping the world.

The issue at stake is the right to speak one's mind.

Recognizing this, many European newspapers reprinted the cartoons. Echoing the story of the defiant slaves, who, when the Romans came for Spartacus, the leader of their rebellion, each proclaimed "I am Spartacus"—this was a clear show of support for the Danish paper and a symbolic affirmation of the right to free speech.

In the United States, however, fear of Muslim anger has suppressed a similar show of support. Indeed, the Bush administration and the mainstream media have generally sided with the raging religionists; while dutifully paying lip service to the First Amendment, their main concern has been for the "hurt feelings" of Muslims. Bush cautioned that we have "a responsibility to be thoughtful about others." Offering similar reasons, major U.S. newspapers like the *New York Times* refuse to print the cartoons. UN Secretary-General Kofi Annan told the world that "of course freedom of speech is never absolute."

Well, is freedom of speech absolute?

Absolutely.

The right to free speech means the right to express one's ideas without danger of coercion, of physical suppression or interference, by anyone. This freedom includes the right to make movies, write books, draw pictures, voice political opinions—and satirize religion. This right flows from the right to think: the right to observe, to follow the evidence, to reach the conclusions you judge the facts warrant—and then to convey your thoughts to others.

To demand special status for any idea or ideology—to declare Judaism or Christianity or Marxism or Islam off-limits, above public criticism—is to negate these rights. No rational mind can function under the order: Follow the evidence wherever you think it leads, but don't you dare come to a negative conclusion about the philosophy of Marxism or the religion of Islam.

The consequence of making submission to authority and not thought—faith, not reason—the sacred value of a society can be observed throughout the Middle East, where censorship, state propaganda, intellectual stagnation, forced compliance with religious edicts and medieval punishments for religious offences are part of everyday life.

Unlike the Muslims now raging across the world, however, many Americans do cherish free speech—yet may be wondering, when so many other Muslims appear to be offended, is this really the issue on which to make an intransigent stand? The answer to this question is unequivocally yes.

Even if it were true that many Muslims are angered by the specific nature of the cartoons, not by the mere fact that Islam was criticized, their anger is irrelevant. Is a Jew to be silenced because Christians find it offensive that he refuses to accept the divinity of Jesus? Or are the Christians to be silenced, because the Jew finds the Trinity offensive? Is the atheist to be silenced, because Jew, Christian and Muslim alike find his ideas offensive? Maybe all the scientific heirs to Galileo should be silenced, as Galileo himself was by the Church, since those who take the Bible literally are angered by the claim that the earth moves?

If we allow anyone's feelings to reign, we destroy freedom of thought and speech.

In a free society, anyone angered by someone else's ideas has a simple and powerful recourse: Don't buy his books, watch his movies, read his newspapers. If one judges his ideas dangerous, argue against them. The purveyor of evil ideas is no threat to those who remain free to counter them with rational ones.

(Note that many European nations have laws limiting free speech, all of which should be repealed; to protest these, however, one does not demand "equal censorship.")

The moment someone decides to answer those he finds offensive with a gun, not an argument—as many Muslims have by demanding that European governments censor the newspapers or by issuing calls for beheadings and other violence against Europeans—he removes himself from civilized society and any rational consideration.

And against this kind of threat to free speech, every free man must stand up. We must vociferously condemn the attempt by religionists to impose censorship in the West. We must extol—without apology or qualifications—the indispensable pillar of a free society: freedom of thought and speech.

The U.S. press should do so by immediately publishing the cartoons, declaring that "I, too, am Spartacus."

The Twilight of Freedom of Speech

Onkar Ghate February 21, 2006

To fathom our government's contemptible treatment of a handful of unbowed journalists, you must see the roots of that treatment in the moral ideal Christianity bequeathed the West.

In the face of the intimidation and murder of European authors, filmmakers and politicians by Islamic militants, a few European newspapers have the courage to defend their freedom of speech: they publish twelve cartoons to test whether it's still possible to criticize Islam. They discover it isn't. Muslims riot, burn embassies, and demand the censorship and death of infidels. The Danish cartoonists go into hiding; if they weren't afraid to speak before, they are now.

How do our leaders respond? Do they declare that an individual's freedom of speech is inviolable, no matter who screams offense at his ideas? No. Do they defend our right to life and pledge to hunt down anyone, anywhere, who abets the murder of a Westerner for having had the effrontery to speak? No—as they did not when the fatwah against Rushdie was issued or his translators were attacked and murdered.

Instead, the U.S. government announces that although free speech is important, the government shares "the offense that Muslims have taken at these images," and even hints that it is disrespectful to publish them.

Why does a Muslim have a moral right to his dogmas, but we don't to our rational principles? Why, when journalists uphold free speech and Muslims respond with death threats, does the State Department single out the journalists for moral censure? Why the vicious double standard? Why admonish the good to mollify evil?

The answer lies in the West's conception of morality.

Morality, we are told incessantly, by secularists and religionists, the left and the right, means sacrifice; give up your values in selfless service to others. "Serve in a cause larger than your wants, larger than yourself," Bush proclaims to a believing nation.

But when you surrender your values, are you to give them up for men you admire, for those you think have earned and deserve them? Obviously not—otherwise yours would be an act of trade, of justice, of self-assertiveness, not self-sacrifice.

You must give to that which you *don't* admire, to that which you judge to be unworthy, undeserving, irrational. An employee, for instance, must give up his job for a competitor he deems inferior; a businessman must contribute to ideological causes he opposes; a taxpayer must fund modern, unemployed "artists" whose feces-covered works he loathes; the United States must finance the UN, which it knows to be a pack of America-hating dictatorships.

To uphold your rational convictions is the most selfish of acts. To renounce them, to surrender the world to that which you judge to be irrational and evil, is the epitome of sacrifice. When Jesus, the great preacher of self-sacrifice, commanded "Love your enemies, bless them that curse you, do good to them that hate you, and pray for them which despitefully use you, and persecute you," he knew whereof he spoke.

In the left's adaptation of this perverse ideal, selfless surrender to evil translates into a foreign policy of self-loathing and "sensitivity," of spitting in America and the West's face while showing respect for the barbarisms of every gang.

Bill Clinton, for instance, certainly no radical leftist, jumped into the recent fray to castigate *us*: "None of us are totally free of stereotypes about people of different races, different ethnic groups, and different religions . . . there was this appalling example in . . . Denmark . . . these totally outrageous cartoons against Islam."

In the right's version, selfless surrender to evil translates into a foreign policy of self-effacing service.

Our duty, Bush declares, is to bring the vote to Iraqis and Palestinians, but we dare not tell them what constitution to adopt, or ban the killers they want to vote for. We have no right to assert our principles, because they are rational and good. But the Iraqis and Palestinians have a right to enact their tribal and terrorist beliefs at our expense, because their beliefs are irrational and evil. In the present crisis, the State Department will not defend free speech, because this principle is rationally defensible; to unequivocally assert this value would be selfish. But the department will suggest that we respectfully refrain from publishing cartoons that upset the mental lethargy of self-made slaves to authority; Muslims have a right to their mystical taboos, precisely because the beliefs are mystical.

Tonight, when you turn on the news and see hatred-seething hordes burning the West's flags and torching its embassies, remember that this is the enemy your morality commands you to love and serve—and remember the lonely Danes hiding in fear for their lives.

And then, in the ultimate act of self-assertiveness, pledge to renounce the morality of sacrifice and learn its opposite: the morality of rational self-interest.

Though the West's twilight has begun, the darkness of suicide has not yet engulfed us. We still have a chance.

The Fear to Speak Comes to America's Shores

Onkar Ghate April 4, 2006

Europeans are all too well acquainted with the fear of criticizing Islam.

To cite just a few of depressingly many examples: a painter, Rashid Ben Ali, is forced into hiding after one of his shows "featured satirical work critical of Islamic militants' violence"; a politician, Ayaan Hirsi Ali, must go underground after it becomes known that she has renounced her Islamic faith; and a film director, Theo van Gogh, is savagely stabbed to death for making a film critical of Islamic oppression of women. And most recently, of course, there were the Danish cartoons. When the *Jyllands-Posten*, in order to expose and challenge this climate of intimidation, printed an article and accompanying cartoons, some of which portrayed Muhammad in a negative light, the response was torched embassies, cries for government censorship, and death threats.

It appears that we should now begin to get used to a similar climate in America.

Borders and Waldenbooks stores have just announced that they will not stock the April–May issue of *Free Inquiry* magazine because the issue reprints some of the cartoons. Is the decision based on disagreement with the content of the magazine? No, not according to Borders Group Inc. spokeswoman Beth Bingham. "For us, the safety and security of our customers and employees is a top priority, and we believe that carrying this issue could challenge that priority."

Borders Group's capitulation to Islamic thugs is understandable given the pathetic response of our and other Western governments.

Has any Western government declared that an individual's freedom of speech is sacrosanct, no matter who screams offense at his ideas? No. Has any Western government proclaimed each individual's right to life and pledged to hunt down anyone, anywhere, who abets the murder of one of its citizens for having had the effrontery to speak? No—as they did not when the fatwah against Rushdie was

---

This article was originally published in the *Bucks County Courier Times*.

issued: American bookstores were firebombed, and Rushdie's translators were attacked and murdered.

On the contrary, our government went out of its way to say that it shares "the offence that Muslims have taken at these images," and even hinted that they should not be published. The British police, Douglas Murray reports, told the editor of a London magazine that they could not protect him, his staff, or his offices from attack—so the magazine removed the cartoons from its website. (A few days later, Murray notes, "the police provided 500 officers to protect a 'peaceful' Muslim protest in Trafalgar Square.")

In the face of such outrages, we must demand that the U.S. government reverse its disgraceful stand and fulfill its obligation to protect our right to free speech.

Freedom of speech means the right to express one's ideas without danger of physical coercion from anyone. This freedom includes the right to make movies, write books, draw pictures, voice political opinions—and satirize religion. This right flows from the right to think: the right to observe, to follow the evidence, to reach the conclusions you judge the facts warrant—and then to convey your thoughts to others.

In a free society, anyone angered by someone else's ideas has a simple and powerful recourse: Don't buy his books, watch his movies, or read his newspapers. If one judges his ideas dangerous, argue against them. The purveyor of evil ideas is no threat to those who remain free to counter them with rational ones.

But the moment someone decides to answer those he finds offensive with a knife or a homemade explosive, not an argument, he removes himself from civilized society.

Against such a threat to our rights, our government must respond with force. If it fails to do so, it fails to fulfill its reason for being: "to secure these rights," Jefferson wrote, "Governments are instituted among Men." And if it fails to do so, we the people must hold it to account.

We must vociferously demand that our government declare publicly that, from this day forward, it will defend by force any American who receives death threats for criticizing Islam—or religion—or any other idea. We must demand that the government protect the stores and employees of Borders, of Waldenbooks, and of any other organization that reprints the cartoons.

We must demand this, because nothing less will prevent America's climate of freedom from disintegrating into Europe's climate of fear.

Surrender in Book on Muhammad Cartoons

Elan Journo September 4, 2009

The *Washington Post* has come out swinging against Yale University Press for deciding to cut visual depictions of Muhammad from a new scholarly book on the Danish cartoons crisis. The book, *Cartoons that Shook the World* by Jytte Klausen, was purged not only of the twelve infamous cartoons, but also of an illustration from a children's book and other artistic depictions of the prophet. None appears in the book, for fear that Islamists may launch attacks in response. The *Post's* editorial observes that the cartoons are "inflammatory and tasteless" but notes that "it's difficult to imagine a more legitimate place for them" than in a scholarly work. By refusing to publish the images, "Yale University Press is allowing violent extremists to set the terms of free speech."

Yes, the decision is a victory for enemies of free speech, but everything in this stinging editorial could be directed right back at the *Washington Post*—and practically every major newspaper in the West that refused to publish the Danish cartoons when that crisis erupted.

If the *Post* believes that the cartoons should be published in a scholarly work analyzing that crisis, why was there no place for them on the pages of the *Post* when the crisis was breaking news? If it is wrong for an academic press to allow Islamists to "set the terms of free speech" today, it was likewise—and perhaps even more—cowardly for the mainstream press back in 2005–06 to allow the brutal mobs to "set the terms of free speech." Freedom of speech cannot be defended only for out-of-the-way scholarly works, while negated and surrendered by major newspapers and media outlets.

In my view the decision of Yale University Press is partly due to the cowardice of the media during the cartoons crisis and since. By failing to stand up for free speech—and failing to demand that our government defend them—the Western media encouraged the Islamist mobs. The mobs (and their leaders) were left to conclude that through intimidation and violent attacks they can coerce Westerners to surrender their right to free speech and obey Islamic dicta against "blasphemy." In the years since, a climate of fear has set in. Few are willing to risk attacks.

What we're seeing today are the results of that fear.

Draw Muhammad, Risk Your Life?

Elan Journo October 6, 2010

Molly Norris was a cartoonist for the *Seattle Weekly*, and although she's still alive, she's gone "ghost": leaving her job, moving, changing her name, and essentially erasing any traces of her identity. For fear of her life.

Exercising her right to free speech—and encouraging others to do the same—she promoted "Everybody Draw Muhammad Day." In July, the Islamist cleric Anwar al-Awlaki (who's linked to the Times Square bomber) announced that Norris "should be taken as a prime target of assassination."(!) Now, at the insistence of the FBI, Norris has gone into the equivalent of a witness protection program—on her own dime.

This scandal has been unfolding for a while . . . so where are the outraged, fire-breathing editorials in our leading newspapers? Where are the impassioned speeches from politicians upholding the inalienable right of Americans to freedom of speech—and specifically, our right to criticize and ridicule ideologies of every stripe? The muted response to Norris's fate, the lack of outrage—particularly from the news media—is horrifying. That our political leaders have pointedly shied away from taking a stand on this is all the more ominous. Government's crucial job is to protect our rights.

Have we sunk so low that drawing Muhammad means risking your life? Is America willing to surrender the fundamental right to freedom of speech in obedience to the dictates of some Islamist cleric?

Freedom of Speech, "Islamophobia," and the Cartoons Crisis

Excerpts from an interview with Flemming Rose.
Elan Journo December 18, 2014

Is there a climate of self-censorship regarding Islam? Has fear led artists and writers to avoid discussion and criticism of Islam? So it seemed to the journalists at *Jyllands-Posten*, Denmark's largest daily paper, in the fall of 2005. To assess the situation, the newspaper invited artists to submit cartoons about Islam. The reaction to the twelve cartoons that were published? Protests, boycotts, deadly riots, attacks on Danish embassies. Some 200 people are thought to have died in the protests. The "cartoons crisis" had gone global.

The aftershocks continued. Just two examples: Yale University Press decided to cut every image depicting Muhammad from a new scholarly book analyzing the cartoon crisis. Kurt Westergaard, the Danish cartoonist who depicted Muhammad with a bomb in his turban, was driven into hiding, escaping two attempts on his life.

What is the situation like today? That was one of the questions I put to Flemming Rose, the editor who commissioned and published the cartoons. He has written a perceptive and riveting new book about the crisis, the reaction to it, and the future of free speech. The book's title hints at the direction of the current trend: *The Tyranny of Silence: How One Cartoon Ignited a Global Debate on the Future of Free Speech.*

Our conversation ranged widely. A few of the issues we touched on: what incidents prompted the commissioning of the cartoons, how self-censorship operated under the Soviet regime and the parallels to today, what lies behind the push to outlaw "defamation of religion," and why the invalid term "Islamophobia" is so destructive.

Below is an excerpt from that interview, edited for inclusion in this book. You can listen to the entire interview (and download the MP3) on our website: bit.ly/tyranny-of-silence

* * *

Elan Journo: *I'm delighted to be speaking today with Flemming Rose about his new book* The Tyranny of Silence: How One Cartoon Ignited a

Global Debate on the Future of Free Speech. *Welcome to the podcast.*

Flemming Rose: It's really a pleasure.

EJ: *What led you to commission the cartoons and then to decide to publish them?*

FR: Some people think that these cartoons came out of the blue, that we just decided to publish some cartoons depicting the prophet, to make a statement or to provoke somebody, or because of other reasons. But in fact they didn't come out of the blue. They were published as a reaction to a sequence of incidents in Denmark, beginning in the middle of September 2005.

At the time a children's author went public, saying, 'I'm writing a book about the life of the prophet Muhammad, but I have problems finding an illustrator.' Two illustrators had turned down the offer to illustrate the book. Finally, one illustrator said yes, but insisted on anonymity, due to fear for possible consequences. When an artist doesn't want to publish something in his own name, that's a form of self-censorship.

The story was on the front page of my newspaper, and several other newspapers. Following up on the story, we had a discussion at my newspaper. One reporter suggested that we find out if there really was self-censorship among people working in the field of culture in Denmark: The idea was to approach illustrators and cartoonists, and ask them to draw the prophet to see how they react. That idea ended on my desk, and so I wrote a letter to all the members of Denmark's cartoonist association inviting them to draw the prophet as they see him—a very open invitation, and that's the reason why in fact the cartoons are so different. I received twelve cartoons.

EJ: *How many people did you approach?*

FR: I approached in fact forty-two people. But I was told in the middle of the process that in fact there were only twenty-five active members of the illustrators association, so about 50 percent replied. At the newspaper, we had a discussion about whether this was enough in order to go on with the project. But when I was told that it was about 50 percent, we thought that it's fine. But we put off publishing the cartoons for about another two weeks, because we had just this one source to this story—the children's writer who said that he couldn't find an illustrator.

While we were discussing those issues at the newspaper, several things happened that convinced me and the other editors that we had to publish those cartoons.

First, the illustrator who had originally insisted on anonymity gave an interview to a Danish newspaper. He acknowledged in public that it was true that he insisted on anonymity because he was afraid. He referred to the fate of Theo van Gogh, a Dutch filmmaker, who was killed on the streets of Amsterdam by a young, offended Muslim in November 2004. The illustrator also referred to the fate of Salman Rushdie, the author of *Satanic Verses*, who was subjected to a fatwah by Ayatollah Khamenei, and had to live in hiding for many years.

Then, at the Tate Gallery, an art museum in London, there was a retrospective by a very famous British avant-garde artist, John Latham. He exhibited an installation called "God is Great." It's a copy of the Bible, Talmud, and the Koran torn into pieces and laid in a piece of glass. The Tate museum decided to remove this piece of art from the exhibition without asking the artist and without asking the curator. There was a similar case at a museum in Sweden, where an artist exhibited a painting depicting a man and a woman having sex, and on the top of the painting was the first verse from the Koran. Again, the director of the museum removed this painting, without asking the artist or the curator.

Another example of self-censorship related to a book by Ayaan Hirsi Ali, a former Dutch politician now residing in the U.S. She had written a collection of essays critical of Islam. Without consulting her, the publisher of the Finnish edition of the book removed a sentence that was seen as maybe offensive to Muslims. Also: several of the European translators of the book insisted on anonymity. Contrary to the usual practice, they did not want to have their name published on the cover or inside the book.

Yet another incident: A Danish stand-up comedian gave an interview to my newspaper in which he said, "you know, I have no problems mocking the Bible in front of the camera, but I'm afraid of doing the same with the Koran." So he was making a clear difference between the way he would treat Christianity when it comes to satire, and the way he would treat Islam.

And then the Prime Minister of Denmark met with a group of Danish imams. This was in the aftermath of the London bombings of July 7, 2005. Two of the imams called on him to influence the Danish press in order to get more positive coverage of Islam, which was basically a call for censorship. It was a call to use the tools of state power in order to get a specific point of view into the press. Both of the imams said this in public after the meeting.

So within the course of one or two weeks, you had several cases all speaking to the same problem of self-censorship when it comes to dealing with Islam in the public space in Denmark and in some other European countries. So we decided that this is a legitimate news story.

You know, in journalism you hear about a problem, and then you want to find out if it's true or not. Usually you would call people and they will tell you what they think about this and that. We just pursued another path, basically following a classic journalistic principle, "Don't tell, show it." So [in writing to the Danish illustrators] we had invited them to show through the medium in which they work to express their opinion, their relationship to this problem.

[Alongside the twelve cartoons we published,] I wrote a short article laying out the background, referring to what I knew about the Soviet Union—that you could end up in prison for ten years for telling a joke in Stalin's Soviet Union—and that this kind of intimidation leads to self-censorship and it's a slippery slope. In this case, we didn't know for sure if this was true or not.

But the events that followed, I think, showed that we really hit a hotspot.

North Korea Threatens Sony;
The President Dithers

In the Sony Affair, Who Is the Real Coward?

Steve Simpson   December 23, 2014

There's something entirely fitting in the fact that the most sensible thing said about Sony's decision not to release the movie *The Interview* comes from a place not known for saying sensible things—Hollywood itself—while the most risible comments come from a place that is supposed to have serious responses to things like foreign nations threatening American citizens for exercising their constitutional rights. That's Washington, D.C. (in case you've forgotten that it's supposed to be a serious place). Comparing the two views expressed is illuminating and goes a long way toward explaining why North Korea felt free to threaten Sony—indeed, all of us—in the first place.

Let's start with the good, which comes from George Clooney in an interview published in *Deadline Hollywood* on December 18, 2014. Unlike most of his colleagues in Hollywood (and commentators everywhere else), Clooney resisted the temptation to blame Sony or to accuse the company of cowardice. Instead, he recognized that Sony would face the risk of serious liability if it released the film.

There's no doubt that Clooney is right about the liability issue. The company that owns the theater in Aurora, Colorado, where a number of people were shot in 2012 during a screening of *The Dark Knight Rises* was sued for allegedly failing to take adequate security measures to prevent the shooting. That was an attack that the theater owners could not have foreseen, yet the judge in the case denied the company's request to dismiss the lawsuits. If movie companies can be liable for an unforeseeable threat of a shooting by a crazy person, there's no question they can be held liable for a known threat of a terrorist attack.

Do the people who have accused Sony and the movie chains of cowardice think they should ignore the threat and face the liability and recriminations that would follow if something happened? Wouldn't many people who are now accusing the companies of cowardice turn on them the moment anything happened and accuse them of shamelessly pursuing profits over people? Many of the same people who are criticizing Sony laughed at the company for weeks because some of its executives wrote embarrassing emails, yet they ignored the impact of the hacking on the company and its employees, and they don't seem to care much about who might be behind it or whether it had any implications beyond Sony. Did Sony's executives have any reason at all to think that if they released the film, anyone would support them?

Clooney picks up on these points as well, noting that the cyberattack is a "terrible" threat to Sony's employees, whose medical records, Social Security numbers, and other personal information was stolen, and that the threat "to blow people up and kill people" is "the actual definition of terrorism."

Yet, "[a]s we watched one group be completely vilified, nobody stood up. Nobody took that stand. Now, I say this is a situation we are going to have to come to terms with, a new paradigm and a new way of handling our business. Because this could happen to an electric company, a car company, a newsroom. It could happen to anybody."

Clooney is right, and what is so refreshing about his comments is that they convey a sense of moral outrage. He recognizes that North Korea's cyberattack and the threats to Sony are an attack on important values—individual employees' rights to privacy, a company's right to carry on its business, everyone's rights to free speech and the freedom to live our lives without the fear of being attacked while watching a movie. And he understands that if no one stands up for these values, they will not last for long.

It's unfortunately more than we can say for the man who is supposed to take the lead in defending these values when they are threatened or attacked by a hostile regime. So let's turn to the bad.

The day after Clooney's interview, President Obama held a press conference in which he did something that is all too common for him: he pointed the finger at someone else. "I'm sympathetic to the concerns that they face," said the president about Sony. But "[h]aving said all that, yes I think they made a mistake." Instead of deciding not to release the film, according to the president, Sony should have called him to ask for advice: "I wish they'd spoken to me first. I would have told them, 'Do not get into a pattern in which you're intimidated by these kinds of criminal attacks.'"

"We cannot have a society in which some dictator some place can impose censorship here in the United States," said the president. To remedy the situation, our government's response will be "proportional" and will come "in a place and time and manner that we choose," he vowed.

It's easy to forget that the man making these comments is the president of the United States. He's the commander-in-chief of our armed forces and the man primarily responsible for deciding how the government will deal with threats against American citizens.

This is a man who has boasted that he has a "pen and a phone" and he knows how to use them. But on this issue, he's acting like he answers phones at the cybersecurity advice hotline. The video of the press conference shows a president who comes off as detached and passive, as if he finds the entire episode boring. Give me a call and I'll offer a few banalities on the situation, but otherwise, why is this my problem?

The president is right that we can't allow dictators to decide what Americans can say and do. But whose job does he think it is to ensure that that doesn't happen? It's not Sony's job, and it can't be; Sony is not the one setting the bad precedent. If a private citizen fails to defend himself against a thug, that sets no precedent about the state of the law. But if the police later refuse to take decisive action against the thug or act like it's not really their problem, that does.

If the president won't take a strong moral stance against North Korea and in defense of Sony, why would we expect anyone else to? It's the president's job to stand up against dictatorships in defense of Americans' rights—indeed, he and the government he leads are the only ones equipped to do so.

Why doesn't our president understand this?

Here's one part of the answer. To exhibit courage and the willingness to act in the face of threats, one must think that whatever is being threatened is actually worth defending. Does President Obama really think anything being threatened in this episode is worth defending? Let's examine the evidence.

What about businesses like Sony? President Obama has spent his entire tenure in office blaming them for every conceivable ill, from the financial crisis to the recession to the alleged problem of income inequality. His administration fined J.P. Morgan Chase after it tried to help the government by taking over Bear Stearns and Washington Mutual, and it sued Standard & Poor's Ratings Services for downgrading the government's credit. He has attacked companies for moving abroad to escape punitive taxation. And he doesn't think that businesses are responsible for their own success. Remember "you didn't build that"?

What about freedom of speech? Well, the president famously scolded the Supreme Court in his 2010 State of the Union address for protecting corporate political speech in *Citizens United*. And he claimed there was nothing to worry about when the IRS under his watch targeted conservative groups for their political speech. And after the Benghazi attack, his administration wasted no time blaming a schlock video, rather than Islamic terrorists.

What about national security and American interests abroad? This is the president who traveled the world after he got into office to, in essence, apologize for American arrogance. He has flip-flopped on foreign policy matters, he has repeatedly caved to Iran's demands over its nuclear program, he regularly criticizes Israel for defending itself against Hamas, and he has continued the American policy of appeasement toward North Korea.

In fairness to President Obama, he is by no means the first president to fail to defend these values. America first reneged on its obligation to defend freedom of speech against terrorist threats in the Rushdie affair under the first President Bush. Then, during the Danish cartoon crisis, our government under Bush II sided with Muslims who were offended by the depiction of Muhammad while those who published the cartoons were facing death threats. And our government's appeasement of terrorists and dictators, including North Korea, goes all the way back to President Reagan, at least.

But the actions of past presidents is no excuse for failing to act properly today, and, in any event, it just affirms my point: our government lacks any real conviction when it comes to defending important American values—indeed, it often attacks those values—and our allies and enemies all know it.

So what *should* the government do about North Korea? There are a number of possibilities, starting with opposing the food aid program to North Korea (which only props up the regime), placing the country back on the list of nations that sponsor terrorism (President Bush was wrong to take it off) and imposing economic sanctions. (Personally, I'd like to see the White House sponsor a double-feature of *The Interview* and *Team America: World Police* on the Mall in Washington, D.C.)

But here's one thing that is indispensable to taking the right actions: having the right convictions and being willing to express them.

North Korea is ruled by a psychopath who leads what amounts to a criminal gang that is systematically starving its own people. It would be a big leap forward if the president—and intellectuals and other politicians—were just willing to say so.

In short, the president should follow George Clooney's lead and express a little moral outrage about this situation and a willingness to stand up for the values that are under attack. It's possible Sony and the theater chains could have shown a bit more spine in this episode—say, by defending themselves a little more forcefully in the press. But until the president and others in Washington are willing to take a firm stance, we shouldn't blame private companies for their unwillingness to face down North Korea alone. Just learning that lesson would help.

Blaming the Victims: The *Charlie Hebdo* and Garland Attacks

Freedom of Speech: We Will Not Cower

Onkar Ghate January 7, 2015

When foreign governments, religious leaders and their faithful followers threaten and murder individuals for daring to speak, anyone who values his own life and freedom must stand with, and speak for, the victims.

We call on everyone to post and publicize the content that these totalitarians do not want us to see, as we have done on our website (and as we did for the cartoons at the heart of the Danish cartoons controversy).

It does not matter whether you agree or disagree with the particular book, cartoon or movie that they seek to silence. We must defend our unconditional right to freedom of thought and freedom of speech.

The totalitarians are counting on self-censorship: that their threats and attacks will leave most of us too scared to speak out and criticize their doctrines. They then have a chance of killing the few individuals brave enough to defy them.

We must end any hope that this strategy will prove effective.

In the wake of the attacks on Sony, many people rightly observed that if *The Interview* were put up on the Internet and made widely available, the attackers' goal of silencing the filmmaker would be unachieved. The same goes for criticism and satire of Islamic doctrine.

If we now all defiantly make the content and images the jihadists wish to ban widely and permanently available across the web, the attackers will have failed. They may have taken the lives of the editor and cartoonists of *Charlie Hebdo*, for which we grieve, but they will not have taken their freedom.

The alternative is to cower and stick our heads in the sand in hope that the issue goes away. But this will not end the threat. It will only make our freedom disappear.

#JeSuisCharlie, but for How Long?

Elan Journo January 12, 2015

The aftermath of the *Charlie Hebdo* attack has brought an encouraging reaction. You can see it on the streets of Paris and other cities. Last week, tens of thousands of people joined vigils in solidarity for the murdered journalists. Upwards of a million Parisians took to the streets on Sunday. "Je Suis Charlie" read the signs. Online the corresponding hashtag has swept across social media. Some news outlets—more than I expected—have reprinted *Charlie Hebdo* cartoons. But what's more, the outlets that have refused to publish the images (or pixelated them) have been deservedly bashed. They shame themselves by cowering.

We are all Charlie—at least today and next week. But what happens once grief and horror naturally attenuate over time?

For the Je Suis Charlie phenomenon to translate into a strengthening of freedom of speech, a great deal depends on the conclusions people form and act on going forward.

Jeffrey Goldberg at *The Atlantic* admonishes that few fully appreciate what it means to stand up for freedom of speech, or have the courage to do so themselves. I'd add: where was the solidarity nearly a decade ago for *Jyllands-Posten*, Flemming Rose, and the artists who were driven in to hiding after the Muhammad cartoons crisis? And before that, after the murder of filmmaker Theo van Gogh? Or, for *Charlie Hebdo* in 2011 when its offices were firebombed?

By now people have many, many more data points. Now, as in the past, the pattern is blatant. The jihadists seek to extinguish the freedom of speech. At *Charlie Hebdo*, the killers declared that they were avenging the prophet. They voiced a standard battle cry, "Allahu Akbar." They executed the journalists during an *editorial* meeting.

The future will bring continuing assaults on the freedom of speech. The courage to defend that freedom presupposes a real *understanding* of it. What's vital now is to champion the freedom of speech, to inform and educate all who will listen. If you value your life and freedom, you should speak up in whatever forum is open to you. Join ARI in our effort to defend the irreplaceable right to the freedom of speech.

Condoning Violence; Destroying Free Speech

Steve Simpson April 29, 2015

In 2015 I gave a talk called "Free Speech Under Siege" at Clemson University in South Carolina, in which I argued that the primary threat to free speech today comes not from terrorist attacks, such as those in Paris in January, but from an unwillingness to defend free speech as a right. That's not to say terrorist attacks aren't significant—ask Flemming Rose or cartoonist Molly Norris how free they feel to speak after being threatened with death for daring to publish drawings of Muhammad. My point is that the threats and killings can only succeed in chilling our speech if we let them. One way we do that is by appeasing those who resort to threats and violence.

Appeasement was on full display after the Paris attacks in what I call the "yes, but" approach to free speech—as in, "yes, free speech is important, but you shouldn't offend someone else's religion" or "violence is not the answer, but how else would we expect people to react to such inflammatory rhetoric?"

Pope Francis took this approach soon after the Paris attacks, calling *Charlie Hebdo* "provocateurs." The Paris attacks obviously were not justified, according to the pope, but "a reaction could have been expected." "You cannot insult the faith of others," he said. The dean of a journalism school displayed the same attitude, writing in *USA Today* that while free speech is important, *Charlie Hebdo*'s mocking pictures of Muhammad were "beyond the limits of the endurable" and therefore outside the protections of the First Amendment.

The latest example of this view comes from Garry Trudeau, author of the popular *Doonesbury* comic strip. Recently, Trudeau took the occasion of winning a lifetime achievement award to criticize *Charlie Hebdo* for publishing "hate speech." He claimed that *Charlie Hebdo* and others who published Muhammad cartoons "provoked" the Paris attacks and other violence across Europe. Unlike the pope, Trudeau didn't even bother to say the Paris attacks were unjustified, but let's be charitable and assume that he doesn't actively support violence against those who draw pictures for a living. Even with that caveat, though, more violence is exactly where his view will lead. The loss of our freedom of speech will be the cost.

After all, to say that someone "provoked" an attack on them is to say that they are at fault and the attacker was justified. Similarly, when someone says, "free speech is important, but you can't offend someone's religion," what he really means is that free speech is not as important as the offended person's feelings.

In either case, the clear message is: the cartoonists are in the wrong, and they, not their attackers, are responsible for the resulting violence. That's what it means to say, as the pope did, that a "reaction could have been expected" and to criticize *Charlie Hebdo* for provoking it. Trudeau made this meaning clear in his own remarks, accusing the cartoonists of "inciting" violence and causing "Muslims throughout France to make common cause with [Islam's] most violent outliers." Islamic terrorism, it turns out, is the fault of a handful of cartoonists and other provocateurs. No wonder the Obama administration blamed a schlock video for the Benghazi attacks.

To be fair to President Obama, this sort of appeasement was going on long before he came along. The first President Bush reacted with little more than annoyance when the Ayatollah Khomeini issued a fatwah against Salman Rushdie for writing *The Satanic Verses*. His son responded to the Danish cartoons controversy by expressing more sympathy for offended Muslims than for cartoonists who were threatened with death.

Is it really surprising that we are getting more violence in response to speech when we've been telling those who resort to it that it works— indeed that it *should* work?

What the appeasers ignore is the vast difference between speech and force. Thomas Jefferson captured the distinction long ago when he said, "it does me no injury for my neighbour to say there are twenty gods, or no god. It neither picks my pocket nor breaks my leg." Speech, no matter how offensive, is fundamentally an appeal to reason and choice. That's true even if the speech in question is not actually reasonable, because the listener always has the choice to stop listening and walk away. Not so when the argument is made with bullets.

It's certainly true that offensive speech—indeed, any speech—can "provoke," but the important question is what is acceptable as a response. Trudeau accuses free speech "absolutists" of failing to recognize an offended group's "right to be outraged. They're allowed to feel pain."

Indeed they are. What they are not allowed to do is respond with violence. In a civilized society, one has the right to respond to speech with anger, outrage, more speech or a cold shoulder. No one has the right to respond with a hail of bullets.

As Ayn Rand once said, "a gun is not an argument." If you doubt that, try debating with someone who agrees to talk to you until you offend them, at which point they will kill you. It's a real conversation stopper.

And, of course, that's the point. Anyone who chooses a gun over an argument wants to control the entire debate—indeed, whether any debate takes place at all. It's senseless to say they just want to prevent "offensive" comments, because a resort to threats and violence means they get to decide what is offensive.

Does anyone really think that people who are willing to respond to cartoons with violence will be satisfied once those cartoons are banned? How does the debate proceed after that point? "You can't draw a picture of my prophet, but feel free to argue that he doesn't exist or that his word isn't law as it says in the Koran"?

What's left when one side in a debate claims the right to control the entire debate and to kill anyone who disagrees with them? Only violence. The irony of all this is that Trudeau, the pope and their fellow critics are the real provocateurs. By condoning violence in response to speech, they will only end up ensuring that violence becomes the rule.

Attacks on Free Speech Come to the U.S.

Steve Simpson   May 5, 2015

In early 2015, there were the attacks on *Charlie Hebdo* in Paris and at a free speech event in Copenhagen. Before that, cartoonist Molly Norris had to go into hiding after launching "draw Muhammad day." That followed threats against Trey Parker and Matt Stone for including Muhammad in episodes of South Park. In 2006 there were the plots against the Danish newspaper *Jyllands-Posten* and death threats against its editor, Flemming Rose, for publishing Muhammad cartoons. The cartoonists, themselves, have all lived in fear of attack since drawing Muhammad. In 2004, Dutch filmmaker Theo van Gogh was murdered for making a film that Muslims found offensive. His collaborator, Ayaan Hirsi Ali, has lived under constant threat of death ever since.

As Peter Bergen argues in a piece for CNN, it was inevitable that one day actual violence over speech that Muslims find offensive would reach our shores.

Now it's happened. On Sunday, two gunmen opened fire at the "Muhammad Art Exhibit and Cartoon Contest" in Garland, Texas. Police shot and killed the two gunmen. One security guard was injured, but it appears the injuries were not serious. We can be thankful for that.

Must Americans now become accustomed to this sort of violence?

Unfortunately, the prognosis is not good. As I wrote on April 29, 2015, many intellectuals in America and elsewhere have taken an attitude of appeasement toward the terrorists and their sympathizers, thus ensuring that their attacks will continue. Of course, violence is not justified, they say, but should we really go out of our way to celebrate those who offend others or humiliate "marginalized" groups? (In this case, the answer is yes.)

Already we are seeing that attitude toward the organizers of the event in Garland, who are being called "Islamophobes" and purveyors of "hate speech," always with the caveat that of course violence is not justified.

But this attitude *is* a form of justifying violence, in the same way that criticizing a rape victim for dressing provocatively is a justification of rape. It says, you brought this on yourself, or you provoked your assailant, or you are the type of person who deserved this. In all events, the message is that your actions, not the actions of your assailants, are the relevant cause of the attack.

There are many circumstances in which it's appropriate not to take sides in a debate or to criticize one side or the other or both. But that applies only when there actually is *a debate* to take sides in or to ignore. It seems too obvious to point out, but a debate does not exist when one side is trying to kill the other.

The moment someone resorts to violence in response to speech is the moment that the issue is no longer about the merits of any side's position or the character of the speakers but about whether we are going to have the freedom to take positions—that is, to think for ourselves—at all. If we fail to support those who are trying to speak, we necessarily end up condoning, and therefore supporting, those who are willing to resort to violence. There's no middle ground in a dispute like this, because there's no middle ground between speech and force. Free speech cannot exist when some people are willing to resort to force.

Whatever one thinks about *Charlie Hebdo* and the organizers of the Garland event or of any of the arguments or positions they take or support, there is no question that Islamists who threaten and use violence want to shut down all debate, all discussion, all thought, and all criticism of their religion. That is why they resort to violence.

If we don't stand against them and in support of those who have the courage to continue criticizing them in the face of threats, then our right to free speech won't be worth much. Eventually, we will lose it. Long before that, we will have deserved to.

Free Speech vs. Religion:
An Interview with Onkar Ghate

The Undercurrent June 23, 2015

*O*nkar *Ghate is a senior fellow and the Chief Content Officer at the Ayn Rand Institute. He has written and lectured extensively on philosophy and serves as dean of the Institute's Objectivist Academic Center in Irvine, California. The Undercurrent's Jon Glatfelter interviewed Ghate about the recent shooting at the "Draw Muhammad" cartoon contest in Garland, Texas, as well as about religion and free speech, more broadly.*

The Undercurrent: *Many of the major U.S. media players, including CNN and FOX, still have not published the cartoon contest's winning piece. Why do you think that is?*

Onkar Ghate: I haven't kept tabs on which outlets have and have not published that cartoon, but there were similar responses in regard to the *Charlie Hebdo* cartoons and, before that, the Danish cartoons in 2005–06. Sometimes a media outlet would try to explain why it is not showing its audience a crucial element of the news story, and I think these explanations have revealed a mixture of motives at work.

Here's a non-exhaustive list: fear, cowardice, appeasement, sympathy. Let me say a word on each. Some media outlets are afraid of violent reprisals and of the ongoing security costs that would be necessary to protect staff. And because the U.S. government refuses to take an unequivocal stand in defense of the right to free speech, the totalitarians are emboldened, which makes violent reprisals more likely. So that's one reason. But despite this legitimate fear, I do think there is often an element of cowardice. The likelihood of an attack can be overstated, and of course if more news outlets publish the cartoons, it is more and more difficult to intimidate and attack them all, and less and less likely that a particular organization will be singled out. Here there is strength in numbers. A third motive is the appeaser's false hope that if he gives in and doesn't publish the cartoons, he will have satisfied the attackers and no further threats or demands will follow. Finally, many are sympathetic: out of deference to the non-rational,

This interview originally appeared on the website of The Undercurrent (theundercurrent.org).

faith-based emotions of Muslims, they don't publish the cartoons, even though those cartoons are news. They view the cartoonists and publishers as the troublemakers and villains. (The roots of this sympathy, I think, are complex and often ugly.)

TU: *Some have condemned the contest's organizer, Pamela Geller, and the winning artist, Bosch Fawstin. They say there's a world of difference between good-natured free expression and malicious speech intended solely to antagonize. What do you think?*

OG: I disagree with many things that I've heard Pamela Gellar say but I refuse to discuss her real or alleged flaws when totalitarians are trying to kill her, as though those flaws, even if real, justify or mitigate the actions of the aspiring killers. The *New York Times* editorial to which you link is a disgrace. After a sanctimonious paragraph saying that we all have the right to publish offensive material and that no matter how offensive that material may be, it does not justify murder, the rest of the editorial goes on to criticize the victim of attempted murder. As my colleague and others have noted, this is like denouncing a rape victim instead of her rapists.

And notice what the editorial glosses over: in the first paragraph, stating that offensive material does not justify murder, it concludes with the seemingly innocuous point that "it is incumbent on leaders of all religious faiths to make this clear to their followers."

This is the actual issue. Why don't you similarly have to tell a group of biochemists or historians, when they disagree about a theory, that their disagreements don't justify murdering each other? The answer lies in the difference between reason and faith, as I'm sure we'll discuss, a difference the editorial dares not discuss.

But contra the editorial, the Garland event had a serious purpose. Look at the winning cartoon: it makes a serious point.

Whether we will admit it or not, there exists today a growing number of totalitarians who seek to impose their version of Islam on the world and to dictate what we in the West can and cannot say. A precedent-setting episode was the fatwah against Salman Rushdie. A foreign leader openly calls for the assassination of a Western author and those involved in the publishing of his book, *The Satanic Verses*, and the U.S. and other Western governments do virtually nothing in response, sometimes worse than nothing.

Fast forward a few years and should it be surprising that there exists a climate of self-censorship with respect to Islam? Western writers, artists and cartoonists are afraid to publish things that might be deemed blasphemous by Muslims. To investigate the extent of the self-censorship in regard to illustrations of Muhammad, the Danish newspaper *Jyllands-Posten* runs a cartoon contest in 2005. Worldwide riots and outrage ensue, death threats proliferate, cartoonists and newspaper editors go into hiding, some are later attacked, and the official Western response to all this is again mostly pathetic.

To me this is a serious problem. There are many other episodes that could be mentioned to drive home the extent of the problem, but a simple way to appreciate its extent is to ask yourself whether you can imagine that instead of the sacrilegious *Book of Mormon* winning over audiences and critics on Broadway, it is the equally sacrilegious musical *The Koran*. Right now, this isn't even in the realm of the possible. Remember what happened when, in the face of the Danish cartoon crisis, Trey Parker and Matt Stone tried to depict Muhammad on *South Park*?

Now in the face of a totalitarian movement that commands us not to utter blasphemous thoughts and threatens us with death if we do, coupled with our own government's appeasing responses, I think it becomes the responsibility of any self-respecting citizen to refuse to cower and for us as a culture to refuse to collapse into self-censorship. Instead, proudly and defiantly utter the blasphemous thoughts. I think a worthy project during the Rushdie years would have been to raise a fund to make his life in hiding easier, purchase the rights to his book for a generous sum, and then publish and distribute millions of copies for free. Similarly with the *Charlie Hebdo* assassinations, I argued that the forbidden cartoons should be plastered all over the Internet. Let it be seen that the attempt to ban these works achieves the opposite. Make it clear that the totalitarian's goal requires killing us all. Declare that I, too, am Spartacus.

I view the Fawstin cartoon as in this same spirit and thus as making a serious, needed point.

TU: *I have friends who want to stand up for free speech but are worried about being labeled "intolerant" by their friends and acquaintances. How do you think everyday citizens should act?*

OG: I've already indicated part of my answer. The totalitarians' goal is to silence us and make us obey. The current tactic is assassination of those who dare speak. The hope is that these attacks will create enough fear to produce widespread self-censorship. Unfortunately, that hope is materializing. Defy them. Put up on your Facebook or Instagram pages the forbidden cartoons and explain that you are purposely doing so in the name of free speech and in order to combat the climate of self-censorship. Or put up links to places that do this, such as ARI.

More generally, among some of the best people today in the West, there is a frightening lack of understanding of the right to free speech, why it is vital, who its enemies are at home and abroad, past and present. Educate yourself about this crucial right and its history, and then try to convince your friends and acquaintances of the importance of the issue.

If you get called names in the process, try to use this as a conversation starter and don't become defensive. Ask the person what he means by "intolerance" and if he can state his actual position. Is his view that we should obey every religious taboo? Many Hindus regard cows as sacred and find it offensive that we eat beef. Should we stop eating beef out of tolerance or respect? Or should we stop doing so only if a group of organized Hindus starts assassinating chefs at steakhouses? Won't this encourage religionists to use violence? Or perhaps his view is that we should not criticize religion? Why not? And does he apply this to all religions, or just Islam? If just Islam, why does it warrant special status?

So my advice is that if you are truly talking about friends and acquaintances with whom you have a positive relationship, treat them as open to persuasion even if they begin by dismissing or belittling your position, politely stand your ground, and discuss and argue.

But of course this presupposes that you have some understanding of the issues involved.

TU: *In a recent panel with Flemming Rose, author of* The Tyranny of Silence, *you said that an individual's right to free speech is one application of a more fundamental right: their right to think. Could you explain that?*

OG: The great battle for freedom in the West was a battle for freedom of thought, including everything this freedom presupposes and everything it leads to. The right to freedom of thought is the right to think for yourself, which means the right to engage in a reasoning process: to gather evidence, logically analyze and weigh it, entertain different arguments, form and follow hypotheses, perform experiments, pursue various lines of questioning, etc., etc. A reasoning process can have no master other than facts and logic. It cannot be subordinate to the approval of a king, pope, president, or fellow citizen, no matter how much they disagree or are offended by what you think. An aspect of this process is to be able to freely discuss and debate ideas with others, and to then present your views and conclusions in an effort to persuade others. Freedom of thought and freedom of speech go together.

Historically, the opponents of freedom of thought and freedom of speech are political authorities operating with the sanction of religion (or some other mystical dogma, like Marxism or Nazism) and religious leaders wielding political power.

TU: *If you view faith and force as intimately linked phenomena, do you see reason and freedom as linked? If so, how has the United States, with its largely Judeo-Christian culture, remained arguably more free than less religious parts of Europe?*

OG: Yes, the connection between faith and force and between reason and freedom is a philosophical issue that some thinkers in the Enlightenment made great strides in identifying and that I think Ayn Rand fully explains.

Very briefly, to extol faith is to extol, in thought and action, blind submission and obedience. As a natural consequence, force will be seen as a means of achieving the good: you can make someone blindly submit and obey by threatening to burn him at the stake or to chop his head off.

But what you *cannot* achieve by the instruments of terror is rational understanding, knowledge, enlightenment. These require that a person himself initiate and direct a process of reason. And this means that if the goal is rational understanding and knowledge, the individual must have the freedom to think and speak. This is why the Age of Enlightenment became the champion of these freedoms.

To answer the second part of the question, the U.S. is not a Judeo-Christian nation. It is the first nation to consciously separate church from state. It is the last, great accomplishment of the Age of Enlightenment and is built on the Greek-Roman achievements that began to be rediscovered during the Renaissance. Nor is it true that Europe is less faith-based than is America. Yes, Americans are overall more overtly religious, but the faith-based doctrines of nationalism, fascism, socialism and communism swept across Europe in a way that they never did in the U.S. Since the time of the American Revolution and its grounding in the Age of Enlightenment, culturally both Europe and America have moved in the direction of mysticism, but Europe has been more mystical than the U.S. and consequently less free.

For a fuller discussion of these issues, you can watch my talks "Religion vs. Freedom" and "The Morality of Freedom."

TU: *In his recent interview with The Undercurrent, Bosch Fawstin labeled himself "anti-Islam." He described Islam as a fundamentally "totalitarian ideology." Is it different from other religions in this respect?*

OG: There is in essence no difference. Any mystical, faith-based doctrine whose leaders are trying to usurp the role of a rational philosophy in human life—as Christians did during the Greek-Roman period, as socialist-Marxists and fascist-Nazis did during the 19th and 20th centuries, and as Islamists are trying to do today—is dictatorial and becomes totalitarian.

Each of these movements is seeking blind submission and obedience to a comprehensive worldview. It should come as no surprise that the daily submission and obedience they desire will eventually be enforced at gunpoint.

This is true of ISIS, of the theocrats in Iran and Saudi Arabia, of the Taliban, of the communists in Russia and China, of Protestants like Calvin and Martin Luther, and of leaders of the Catholic Church.

TU: *A widely held view is that Islam, to say nothing of the world's other major religions, is peaceful. In fact, immediately post-9/11, President George W. Bush described Islam as a religion "of peace" that has been "hijacked." Do you agree?*

OG: Like much of what comes out of George W. Bush's mouth, this is the opposite of the truth. As I've already indicated, the essence of religion, namely faith, sanctions the use of force. If blind submission and obedience are the goals, coercion is an effective means. A worldview accepted on faith encourages not peace but war. Centuries of religious conflict and warfare are not some inexplicable accident.

Also no accident is that the greatest of America's Founding Fathers, Jefferson and Madison, deliberately separated church from state. They did so partly in the name of peace. Let us live under principles and laws whose origin is reason, not blind faith, and we can all rationally agree to them and live peacefully together.

TU: *It seems that free expression is under assault on a number of fronts today. What does this issue of free speech mean to you personally? Why have you chosen to dedicate a significant portion of your scholarship to defending it?*

OG: Because of their viewpoints, many of the Enlightenment's thinkers were on the run from the political and religious authorities. But they eventually won and put an end to such arbitrary power. It is an enormous accomplishment and an enormous gift, not to be surrendered.

I'm an intellectual. My entire career revolves around the reasoned investigation and communication of philosophical ideas and theories, ideas and theories that others often find offensive. If I won't stand up for my right to freedom of thought and speech, and fight for these, I have no business calling myself an intellectual. And I have no business professing admiration for Locke, Jefferson, Madison and other heroes of freedom, if I stand idly by as people try to smash their achievements.

TU: *Do you have any recommendations for those who want to explore the topics of free speech and religion in more depth? Can we expect any future projects or events on these issues from you or the Institute?*

OG: I've already mentioned a few things of mine and of others at ARI that people can read and watch. Flemming Rose's book, to which you linked, is also definitely worth reading. For those who don't know, he was the editor who published the Danish cartoons; I admire his benevolence and courage.

In a few weeks I will be speaking at our summer conference, where I will address some of these issues in more detail, including some issues that we did not have time to touch on today. The talk's titled *"Charlie Hebdo, the West and the Need to Ridicule Religion."* I hope to see some of your readers there!

And of course in the months and years to come, look to ARI to continue to uphold and defend the individual's right to freedom of thought and speech.

Cheering for the *Charlie Hebdo* Attacks: The Shape of Things to Come?

Elan Journo October 6, 2015

Ten years ago last week, the Danish newspaper *Jyllands-Posten* published twelve cartoons related to Islam. The aim was to gauge a seemingly growing climate of self-censorship in Europe. The ensuing crisis went global.

By looking at the erosion of free speech in Europe, you could see markers of what to expect here. European self-censorship, my colleague Onkar Ghate argued at the time, was coming to America. By the spring of 2006, Borders Books and Waldenbooks announced that they would not stock an upcoming issue of *Free Inquiry* magazine, because it reprinted some of the notorious cartoons.

The fear was pervasive. Major American news outlets refused to reprint the cartoons, even in reports on the rioting and deaths related to the cartoons crisis. Some years later, Yale University Press published a scholarly book analyzing the cartoons crisis—but decided just before going to press to excise every one of the twelve cartoons, along with other images.

In Europe, filmmakers, artists, and writers had been threatened, attacked, murdered. Such threats and attacks were occurring here too.

In January 2015: Islamist gunmen massacred journalists at the magazine *Charlie Hebdo* in Paris. In May 2015: Islamists tried to attack a free speech event in Garland, Texas. Writing on *Voices for Reason*, Steve Simpson pointed out that the destruction of freedom of speech succeeds in large part because of the continuing appeasement in the West of those who resort to threats and violence. Steve's post, incidentally, was published five days before the Garland attack.

Although Europe is farther along, the trend is clear. That's what came to mind when I read Brendan O'Neill's account of a debate at the prestigious Trinity College, Dublin, in Ireland, on the right to be offensive. He writes:

> I was on the side of people having the right to say whatever the hell they want, no matter whose panties it bunches. The man on the other side who implied that *Charlie Hebdo* got what it deserved, and that the right to offend is

a poisonous, dangerous notion, was one Asghar Bukhari of the Muslim Public Affairs Committee.

It is depressing, but not surprising, that Bukhari's view is taken seriously.

What I found bone-chilling is the reaction of students in the audience. They listened intently to Bukhari's case. Some cheered.

"This is how screwed-up the culture on Western campuses has become," writes O'Neill. "I was jeered for suggesting we shouldn't ban pop songs; Bukhari was cheered for suggesting journalists who mock Muhammad cannot be surprised if someone later blows their heads off."

One audience at one debate at one university in one city: obviously that's at most a data point, not a trend. But do the attitudes of these students—whom O'Neill describes as non-fringe, young, and with-it—reflect broader trends in Europe? Quite possibly.

What does that imply for the future of free speech in Europe—and here?

In the San Bernardino Attacks, a Stark Example of the Difference Between Speech and Crime

Steve Simpson December 10, 2015

G iven that there are so many people today who believe that offensive speech ought to be outlawed, it's worth rehearsing the crucial legal and moral difference between free speech and murder. In a column that might be described as picking over the body of one of the San Bernardino victims for evidence that he deserved it, Linda Stasi of the New York *Daily News* inadvertently provides us with a valuable comparison that illustrates this difference. Stasi reviews the beliefs of the terrorists and one of their victims, Nicholas Thalasinos, a religious conservative who often harshly criticized Islam, and declares them all to be hateful bigots. The implication, which Stasi isn't willing to state openly, is that Thalasinos and his killers are in some sense morally equivalent and that people who harshly criticize Islam—Stasi mentions Pamela Geller as an example—are, at least in part, the cause of Islamic terrorism. This view, which was abundant among intellectuals on the left after the *Charlie Hebdo* and Garland, Texas, attacks, manages to obliterate the moral and legal distinction between the terrorists and their victims and to blame the victims in the process.

I should point out that I think Nicholas Thalasinos had some nutty and odious views. He considered abortion to be murder and repeatedly accused Planned Parenthood of the crime. He claimed that Hillary Clinton is a eugenicist because she described herself as a progressive who supports the right to abortion. (There were many supporters of eugenics among 19th- and early 20th-century progressives, but that doesn't make Hillary Clinton one.) And he believed in his own form of religious fundamentalism.

Of course, as an atheist, I think all religions, including Islam, are fundamentally irrational and wrong. I don't know enough about either Christianity or Islam to say that the latter is more irrational or violent in principle than the former, but it's clear that a significant percentage of Muslims today (certainly throughout the Muslim world) follow their religion to the point of condoning or committing terrorism and murder. The same is simply not true of today's Christians and Jews, however. *Why* that is so is an important question. *That* it is so is obvious. (For more on this general topic, see Elan Journo's book *Winning the Unwinnable War*, among other things he's written.)

But having and expressing odious ideas is not the same thing as committing murder. Even if we grant that some of Thalasinos's ideas were just as irrational as the ideas of the people who murdered him, there's still a world of difference between Thalasinos and his killers. The San Bernardino terrorists chose to impose their views on others by *force*—by killing and injuring them and terrorizing an entire nation (which was their goal). Thalasinos chose to use *persuasion*. He tried to convince others that he was right by speaking and arguing. By all accounts, Thalasinos was a civil, albeit outspoken, person. He agitated for his religious and political views and against Islam, but otherwise left people alone to live their lives. The same cannot be said about his killers. As we now know, one of them pledged allegiance to ISIS, a known terrorist group. For months, both participated in a conspiracy to commit at least one terror attack. That they were soft-spoken parents of an infant child who minded their own business right up until they committed mass murder is of no consequence in judging them, morally or legally. By ignoring this crucial difference—that Thalasinos respected the rights of others, but his killers did not—Stasi obliterates the difference between peaceful, law-abiding citizens and criminals.

This difference is absolutely crucial to the existence of a free and civilized society. In a free society, people are entitled to believe and say all sorts of offensive and disagreeable things. What they are not free to do is impose those views on others at the point of a gun. Initiating force against others is a monstrous evil. It prevents people from thinking for themselves, acting on their own judgment, and pursuing their own happiness. Ultimately, it prevents them from *living*, a point that was demonstrated to terrifying effect in the San Bernardino attacks.

The basic condition of living in a free society is renouncing the use of force in favor of reason and persuasion. Even people with irrational and odious ideas can observe this line and respect the rights of others. Millions of people do. By all accounts, Nicholas Thalasinos did. That made him a civilized, law-abiding person. Refusing to observe the line between force and persuasion made his killers barbarians.

In ignoring the difference between the two, Stasi and others who engage in tacit victim-blaming ignore the fact that terrorists, like everyone else, are able to *choose* their actions and therefore bear responsibility for those actions. They don't have to resort to violence. They could do what Nicholas Thalasinos did and speak instead.

Implicitly, Stasi's view amounts to the idea that "hateful" speech *causes* others to resort to violence. The offended and outraged are not really responsible for their actions, according to this view. They are driven by their passions and the sense of powerlessness and oppression inspired by the "hatred" and "bigotry" of their critics. As a result, it's the "hatred" and "bigotry" on which we should focus in the aftermath of deadly attacks and terrorism, not the evil choices of the perpetrators.

Cartoonist Garry Trudeau expressed this view after the Paris attacks. *Charlie Hebdo* was "punching downward" at a "powerless, disenfranchised minority," he said. The publication's offensive speech caused Muslims in Europe to join with radicals, and "incited" riots and violent protests throughout the Muslim world. The killers and those who supported and condoned their actions were not fundamentally at fault, under this view. The real culprits were those who "provoked" them with offensive ideas.

Notice that this approach denies moral agency to the very people who are claimed to be the victims. They are like a pack of hungry wolves being taunted with fresh meat. If they attack, it's not them we should blame, but "haters," like Pamela Geller, *Charlie Hebdo*, and now Nicholas Thalasinos, who inflame their passions by criticizing their religion.

If we accept this view, how can we draw a distinction in law between those who murder and those who merely speak out? If people are driven by their passions or their feelings of "powerlessness" to commit crimes, if offensive speech causes them to lash out, if those who respect the rights of others by using words instead of bullets can be lumped together as "haters" and "bigots" with those who murder and terrorize, how can we justify treating one group differently than the other? Why do we label one group "murderers" and the other "innocents"? The logical answer is that there really is no difference between them, and they *should* be lumped together. We should, in effect, forgive one group for their sins (because they're not really responsible) and shift the blame to the other or to "society" in general.

By ignoring the crucial moral distinction between those who choose to initiate force against others and those who don't, we end up blurring the legal distinction between free speech and murder (indeed, between any non-violent behavior and a deadly assault). We end up where Garry Trudeau and many others have ended up: equating speech that offends with incitement, threats, and other criminal behavior. It's not surprising that with this attitude come demands (on college campuses among other places) to ban speech that offends people.

Of course, as a practical matter, the difference between initiating force and communicating ideas is not always obvious. It's easy enough to tell the difference between someone who commits murder by his own hand and someone who engages in a debate (at least it should be). But how do we know when someone has committed the crime of incitement? Why isn't Trudeau correct when he claims that *Charlie Hebdo* "incited" millions of Muslims to riot and commit crimes?

The law of incitement is a big subject. The simplest answer I can give is that incitement is similar to crimes like conspiracy and aiding and abetting criminals. All of them require, in essence, a conscious and intentional plan to initiate force against others and positive steps toward that end. The perpetrator has to do more than say something that angers or offends people, who then go off and commit crimes on their own. In effect, he has to be trying to convince them to join with him to violate the rights of others.

For a very good, albeit grim, example of incitement, conspiracy, and threats all wrapped up in one publication, I refer you to Al Qaeda's terrorist recruitment magazine, *Inspire*. One issue (images of which you can find on line) calls for the deaths of a number of people who have offended Islamists over the years (Flemming Rose and Ayaan Hirsi Ali among them). There's evidence that the San Bernardino terrorists may have found instructions for the pipe bombs they made in this publication.

There's a very big difference between what *Inspire* and the San Bernardino killers have done, on the one hand, and anything Pamela Geller, *Charlie Hebdo*, or Nicholas Thalasinos have done, on the other. We ignore that difference at our peril.

"Je Suis Charlie" No Longer: A Year After the Attacks, Is the West Betraying Free Speech?

Steve Simpson January 7, 2016

One year ago today, Islamic terrorists entered the offices of the French publication *Charlie Hebdo* and fired sixty shots inside of three minutes. When the smoke cleared, eleven employees of the magazine and one building maintenance worker had been killed, and eleven other people in the building had been injured. The "crime" for which these individuals were being punished was blasphemy. The magazine had offended Islamists by publishing images of Muhammad. It had done so often over the years, but *Charlie Hebdo*'s satire was not aimed exclusively at Islam. The magazine was an equal opportunity offender. It lampooned Muslims, Christians, Jews, and many others with equal vigor.

No longer. Six months after the attack, *Charlie Hebdo* announced that it would stop publishing images of Muhammad. Around the same time, cartoonist Renald Luzier, who drew covers for *Charlie Hebdo*, announced that he, too, would stop drawing the Islamic prophet.

Can we blame them?

Another Frenchman, Voltaire, is widely believed to have said "I disapprove of what you say, but I will defend to the death your right to say it." The line, in fact, comes from a biographer who was attempting to summarize Voltaire's view, but it no doubt accurately expresses what the French philosopher believed, and it certainly reflects the spirit of the Enlightenment in which he lived. Free speech is so important that we ought to be willing to lay down our lives to defend it.

Voltaire and the other thinkers of the Enlightenment were well aware that free speech, and its corollary, free thought, are essential to a free and civilized society. They lived at a time in which the Western world had only recently emerged from centuries dominated by superstition and brute force. It was a world ruled by the earthly interpreters of imaginary creatures—"gods"—that they claimed had granted them divine authority to treat the rest of humanity like sacrificial animals. But because superstition and force produce nothing but death and destruction, that world was marked by crushing poverty, sickness, violence, despotism, and perpetual war. That is the world to which the

Islamic terrorists who attacked *Charlie Hebdo* would very much like to return us.

A world like that has no room for the free-thinking individual. He is a constant threat to the popes and potentates who live by faith and thus always end up ruling by force. Theirs is a world governed by commandments issued to supplicants and slaves. It requires obeisance and submission. Free-thinking individuals do not submit. They question, they discuss, they debate, they use reason to pursue the evidence to wherever it leads them.

To be sure, those who embrace free thought and free speech don't always produce knowledge or speak articulately. But theirs is the only method that allows us to understand the world so we may reap all the benefits it has to offer. The last three hundred years are a testament to what freeing man's mind from the shackles of superstition and faith produces: health, wealth and prosperity on a scale that the world has never known. Without the freedom to think and to pursue knowledge, to question prevailing views, to share information, and to communicate our thoughts, the modern world would not be possible.

Still, as important as free thought and free speech are, it is one thing to say you will risk your life to defend them, but quite another actually to do so.

The employees of *Charlie Hebdo* did so. No doubt, risking their lives was not their goal. But years of death threats and a bombing in 2011 had to have made them aware of the risk that continuing to publish images of Muhammad carried. Still, they persevered.

Now they have stopped publishing those images. Their editor, Laurent Sourisseau, denies that the attacks last January had anything to do with the decision, but that defiant claim does not ring true. He insists, almost as an apology, that the magazine will still criticize religions, but that is rather like saying one will continue to criticize malcontents without singling out those who are committing murder. The current issue, published to commemorate the attacks, gives us a glimpse of what he means. The cover depicts a blood-spattered generic God with an AK-47 slung over his shoulder above the caption: "One year later, the assassin is still out there." While there is certainly ample reason to criticize all religions today, the fact remains that it is the Islamists who regularly sling AK-47s over their shoulders and shoot innocent people. Most of the other religions have a long and bloody history behind them, but today, it is only the adherents of the Islamist movement who are waging a jihad against the West and putting to death those who flout their dogmas. And, of course, it was the Islamists who threatened *Charlie Hebdo* and finally made good on those threats. The one-year anniversary of that attack would seem an odd time to decide that all religions are equally responsible for that sort of violence.

The reluctant conclusion to which I'm drawn is that *Charlie Hebdo* has been frightened into muting its criticisms. It claims the right to criticize all religions, but there seems little doubt, as its decision not to publish images of Muhammad shows, that it will no longer exercise that right with quite the same zeal that it once did. Islamists have succeeded in blunting *Charlie Hebdo*'s pen.

I'll ask again, should we blame *Charlie Hebdo* for this decision?

To answer that question, let's consider the moral landscape in which the publication operated. Start in 1989, when Iran's Ayatollah Khomeini issued a fatwah against Salman Rushdie for allegedly offending Islam in his book, *The Satanic Verses*. The Bush administration muttered some words of protest, but neither it nor any other Western nation took any action in response. Rushdie has lived in hiding ever since. That was the Islamists' first victory in their perpetual war against free thought and free speech. It would not be their last.

Most people are familiar with the major incidents: Theo van Gogh, the Dutch filmmaker, murdered in broad daylight in 2004 for making a film that offended Islamists; Ayaan Hirsi Ali, his collaborator and an outspoken critic of Islam, threatened with death in van Gogh's attack (in a note pinned to van Gogh with a dagger) and forced to live under tight security ever since; the Danish cartoons controversy, in which Muslims the world over erupted in protest after a newspaper, *Jyllands-Posten*, published a number of cartoons depicting Muhammad; the 2010 plot against the creators of *South Park* for showing Muhammad dressed as a bear in an episode of the show; Molly Norris, who left her life as a cartoonist in Seattle and went into hiding after she became the subject of death threats for initiating a "draw Muhammad day" in response to the *South Park* controversy; and, of course, the attack on *Charlie Hebdo* last year, and, a few months later, the attack on Pamela Geller's "Draw Muhammad" contest in Garland, Texas.

But these are only a few of the threats and attacks on those who have spoken in ways that offend Islamists. How many people know that Kurt Westergaard, who drew perhaps the most infamous cartoon in the controversy—the one showing Muhammad wearing a bomb instead of a turban—was attacked in his home by an axe-wielding

Muslim man who evaded a surveillance system and hacked through a door while Westergaard babysat his granddaughter? Westergaard escaped injury by retreating to a safe room that had been built for just that purpose. Who remembers Lars Vilks, the Swedish artist who drew a picture of Muhammad's head on a dog's body? Police foiled plots to kill him in 2010 and 2014, but Vilks was again attacked by gunman while participating in a forum about free speech at a cafe in Denmark. He escaped unharmed, but one person was killed and several others were wounded. That shooting happened in February, so it was lost amid all the attention devoted to the *Charlie Hebdo* attack.

And how many people know that *Jyllands-Posten* editor Flemming Rose decided to publish the cartoons, as part of an issue devoted to examining self-censorship, after he learned that the author of a children's book on the life of Muhammad could find no illustrators willing to draw the prophet? All the artists solicited were unwilling to risk becoming the next Rushdie or Theo van Gogh. Who is aware of the recriminations Rose faced after publishing the cartoons or the fact that Ayaan Hirsi Ali was effectively driven from her adopted homeland of Holland after a controversy developed over whether the government should provide for her security, and everywhere she lived, neighbors complained that they feared for their safety? Rose provides many more examples of threats, self-censorship, and appalling appeasement and fear among Western intellectuals in his book *The Tyranny of Silence*.

Each of these people was trying to focus attention on an important issue, whether it was the threat to free speech posed by Islamists, the horrific treatment of women under Islam, or the growing threat of terrorism from the Islamic world. What we learned from the controversies they sparked was something just as dispiriting: a surprising number of Western intellectuals and opinion leaders are not willing to defend free speech and many oppose it outright. Governments, too, have been unwilling to defend this important right (or to act decisively against terrorism in general).

Of course, no one is quite willing to admit that openly. But the view that free speech is not terribly important and should typically yield to the feelings of others was present in the reactions to almost every attack. Typically it is conveyed by expressing far more sympathy for offended Muslims than for the victims of Islamist attacks. President George W. Bush took exactly that approach when he rushed to express his concern for offended Muslims after the Danish cartoon crisis and his State Department compared the cartoons to racial slurs. "We find [the cartoons] offensive, and we certainly understand why Muslims would find these images offensive." The State Department added that "Anti-Muslim images are as unacceptable as anti-Semitic images . . . as anti-Christian images, or any other religious belief."

This argument is a dodge. Certainly, there are all sorts of images of racial, ethnic, and religious groups that can legitimately be described as offensive. But in assessing that, one key question is, do they convey something that is true? Images of Jews sucking the blood from Palestinian children or orchestrating a worldwide banking conspiracy are offensive because they are viciously false. But if Jews en mass began invoking their religion as grounds for murdering innocent people and threatening and killing those who criticized them, I would look forward to cartoons showing them with bombs beneath their yarmulkes. Cartoons are a good way to make an important point succinctly, and anyone who engages in terrorism *should* be criticized (at a minimum).

The idea that the religious beliefs of anyone, terrorists or otherwise, are somehow beyond criticism is crazy. Religion is a body of ideas that is supposed to act as a guide to action, and the religious invoke it as such all the time. If there is reason to believe that a given religion is being used to justify murder and terrorism, then of course we should question, criticize, and even ridicule it and its followers (indeed, given the fundamental irrationality of religion—it is admittedly based on faith, after all—religion should be criticized even when its adherents are not invoking it to commit murder). When certain Christian sects invoke their religion to refuse necessary medical treatment for their children (vaccines, for example), we criticize and even mock them. Why wouldn't we respond similarly to Islamists who invoke their religion to justify using children as walking bombs?

We saw this same approach after the *Charlie Hebdo* attacks. First, Pope Francis called the magazine's editors "provocateurs" and suggested that the magazine had gotten what it deserved. "[A] reaction could have been expected," said the pope. "You cannot insult the faith of others." Did he mean that *Charlie Hebdo* should have expected a hail of gunfire and the murder of eleven employees in response to publishing cartoons? It's not clear; the pope's main concern was expressing sympathy for the faithful whose feelings had been hurt.

Next, a journalism professor, writing in *USA Today*, argued that the images printed in *Charlie Hebdo*—those goofy cartoonish pictures of Muhammad—were "beyond the limits of the endurable" and therefore "fighting words" that were not protected under the First Amendment. His legal argument is wrong, but notice the implicit view that any Muslim viewing these cartoons could not help but to riot and kill.

This was a theme that returned time and again after the *Charlie Hebdo* and Garland, Texas, attacks. Cartoonist Garry Trudeau invoked the image of Muslims driven mad by rage when they saw their prophet ridiculed. He accused *Charlie Hebdo* of "punching downward" at a "powerless, disenfranchised minority" and thereby "inciting" riots throughout Europe. A group of authors made the same claim when they protested the decision of the writers group PEN to present an award for courage to *Charlie Hebdo*, calling the magazine's criticisms of Islam "culturally intolerant" and "Islamophobic." The *New York Times* trotted out the "Islamophobe" epithet in a scathing editorial after the Garland, Texas, attack that was primarily aimed, not at the terrorists, but at Pamela Geller, who organized the event. Writing in *Bloomberg*, Harvard law professor Noah Feldman argued that Geller was morally responsible for the shootings because it was foreseeable that they would occur. Indeed, the possibility of a shooting was certainly foreseeable, which is the reason Geller hired security guards at the event—who, we should be happy to note, did their jobs very effectively in dispatching the attackers before they reached the building. But keep in mind that the attack was foreseeable only because *this is how Islamists act*. Feldman's argument amounts to what James Taranto of the *Wall Street Journal* has referred to as the "assassin's veto." The more likely it is that your opponents will attack you, the more morally culpable you are for exercising your right to criticize them. As a result, you should just shut up.

To summarize these critics' views is to illustrate just how vicious and absurd they truly are. If we mock or satirize those who kill innocent people that is unjust "cultural intolerance" or "punching downward" at a "powerless minority" (not so powerless that they are unable to kill those who offend them, of course). To suggest that their violent behavior is motivated by the religion that they, themselves, constantly invoke to justify their evil deeds is to indulge an irrational fear. Yet, at the same time, because everyone knows the Muslim world is prone to outbursts of violence, we are obliged to predict that some of them will explode with rage at the slightest provocation. But if it is really true that many Muslims are so prone to violent outbursts, then why is it unjust or irrational to mock and criticize them?

Muslims, under this view, are like a pack of wild animals. Taunt them and you are sure to get mauled. It's not their fault; that's just how wild animals behave. Indeed, it is worse than this. If we were dealing with wild animals, we would not be criticized for saying so. With Islamists, we are supposed to know that they are dangerous, but we are not supposed to admit it, because that would be "culturally intolerant."

This is, of course, rubbish. Muslims are as able to make rational choices as anyone else. If they choose to commit terrorist acts, they should be held accountable like anyone else would be. Those among them who condone terrorism or violence should be held accountable as well—at the very least, by being criticized for their views, including their religious views. And, yes, that criticism should often take the form of mockery and satire, which are wonderful ways of puncturing bad ideas and the often pompous and irrational individuals who hold them.

But this is not what Western intellectuals have done. They express shock and dismay at terrorist attacks, but their criticisms always come with caveats. "Of course, violence is not justified, but . . ." or "Of course, speech is important, but . . ." Inevitably, the "buts" are followed by "we should expect this sort of reaction" or "no one should criticize another person's religion." This means that violence *is* in some sense justified and freedom of speech does not really mean *freedom* of speech. It means something more like toleration of speech as long as it doesn't go too far. That is not criticism of terrorism; it's appeasement. And it's not a defense of free speech, but a capitulation to those who attack it.

Should it surprise us, then, that a world-weary Laurent Sourisseau, in announcing *Charlie Hebdo*'s decision not to publish images of Muhammad any longer, said, "We have drawn Muhammad to defend the principle that one can draw whatever they want [. . . .] It is a bit strange though: We are expected to exercise a freedom of expression that no one dares to."

I would add: and for which you are criticized for having the courage to exercise.

Let us restate the original question: Can we blame *Charlie Hebdo* for its decision to stop courting death in order to exercise a right that few others in the media, among intellectuals, and even in government seem to care about and for which *Charlie Hebdo* was constantly criticized?

The answer is simple.

No individual or group of individuals can be expected to continue exercising a right when they have no assurance that they will be protected from attack for exercising that right. Obviously, it is government's job to provide that protection, and the growing number of individuals who have been attacked or threatened for speaking out or have given up doing so entirely is a sad commentary on the failure of their governments to protect them. But we must ask why this has happened. It isn't a lack of resources or something that makes Islamic terrorism uniquely difficult to combat, but a lack of conviction that we, and our values, are worth protecting. Western intellectuals are abandoning the values of free speech and free thought (indeed, all Enlightenment values) and governments, not surprisingly, are following suit.

Values like free speech and freedom of thought will remain common values only if they are treated as such. Part of treating them as values means having the moral courage to defend them. The employees of *Charlie Hebdo* exhibited that moral courage. They exercised their right to free speech when it mattered—indeed, when most others in the media lacked the courage to do so. This made the publication more than just a satirical magazine. In its defiance of the Islamists, *Charlie Hebdo* became a standard-bearer for the principle of free speech. Far from blaming the publication for anything, we ought to commemorate the attacks on it by praising its employees for bravely carrying that burden as long as they did. That is so no matter what we think of the content or quality of what they publish.

Still, we ought to lament the hit that freedom of speech has taken this year—in the terrorist attacks and the shameful reactions to them in the West; in the failure of governments to protect this important right; in *Charlie Hebdo*'s decision to stop publishing images of Muhammad; in the animosity toward free speech that college students and many intellectuals increasingly display.

Is there any good news?

Yes. A kind of visceral support for free speech remains embedded in the American psyche, as far as I can tell, at least outside of intellectual circles. And there are still many intellectuals who are willing to defend the right to free speech. Flemming Rose remains indefatigable despite living under the constant threat of attack. The same is true of Ayaan Hirsi Ali. Pamela Geller is a tenacious advocate for free speech. Bosch Fawstin, whose drawing won the contest in Garland, Texas, remains defiant. And we at ARI will continue to fight for this important right.

The Consequences of Appeasement: A Timeline of Attacks on Free Speech

The Rushdie Affair

December 1988–January 1989: Viking Penguin, the American publisher of Salman Rushdie's book *The Satanic Verses,* receives thousands of threatening letters and several bomb threats.

February 14, 1989: Ayatollah Khomeini of Iran issues a fatwah (religious edict) demanding the death of Salman Rushdie, who goes into hiding under police protection.

February 14–18, 1989:

- Viking Penguin and many bookstores receive death threats. A bomb threat leads the publisher to close its Manhattan office temporarily.
- Fearing attacks, three major North American bookstore chains—B. Dalton Booksellers, Waldenbooks and Coles Book Stores Ltd. of Canada—pull *The Satanic Verses* from the shelves of more than 2,600 stores.
- Small booksellers across North America follow suit.

February 21, 1989: President George H. W. Bush's reaction was appeasing: "However offensive that book may be, inciting murder and offering rewards for its perpetration are deeply offensive to the norms of civilized behavior." With that shameful statement, Bush implied that Khomeini and Rushdie were equally objectionable. Bush added a pro forma warning that America would hold Iran "accountable" should any action be taken against U.S. interests—as if the attack on the principle of freedom of speech and the incitement to murder had no bearing on our interests. Taking no action against Iran, Washington bowed in deference to a blood-lusting Islamic theocrat and sacrificed the freedom of Americans.

February–December 1989:

- Two bookstores in Berkeley, California are firebombed.
- During the first half of the year, Viking Penguin reportedly spends nearly $3 million on security.
- In March alone, FBI registers more than seventy-five threats to bookstores; B. Dalton Bookseller received thirty in under three hours.

- Bookstore at Dulles Airport posts sign: "We do not stock *The Satanic Verses*"; another bookseller omits it from displays of top-ten best-sellers.

- One French publishing company is put under 24/7 police guard; other European publishers delay release of translations of *The Satanic Verses*

- Few British booksellers stock the book; some offer it, but under the counter.

July 1991: The Italian translator of *The Satanic Verses* is stabbed, but survives. The Japanese translator is knifed to death.

Submission (2004 film)

August 19, 2004: *Submission*, a short film directed and produced by Theo van Gogh and written by Ayaan Hirsi Ali, airs on the Dutch public broadcasting network (VPRO). The film points to the Koran as a rationale for the oppression of women in Islam.

November 2, 2004: An Islamist brutally murders Theo van Gogh on an Amsterdam street. Van Gogh's "crime," according to a note pinned to his body, was making a critical film about Islam. The note also promised to punish other "blasphemers" involved in the film, including Ayaan Hirsi Ali, who now lives under round-the-clock security.

The Danish Cartoons Crisis

September 30, 2005: *Jyllands-Posten*, Denmark's largest daily newspaper, publishes twelve cartoons of the prophet Muhammad.

September–December 2005: A group of imams foment opposition to *Jyllands-Posten* within Denmark, including a veiled threat of violence. They exert pressure on the Danish prime minister to demand an apology from the newspaper and seek support from Muslim regimes.

January–February 2006:

- The twelve cartoonists; Carsten Juste, editor in chief; and Flemming Rose, culture editor, at *Jyllands-Posten* receive death threats.

- A Pakistani cleric offers a bounty of $1 million for the heads of the cartoonists.

- Attacks on Danish embassies in Syria, Iran, Pakistan, Lebanon.

- Violent protests in Afghanistan, Malaysia, Indonesia, Pakistan, Libya, Turkey.

- Boycotts of Danish products, endorsed by several Muslim countries.

- At least two hundred deaths attributed to the protests, riots, bombings.

- Some European newspapers, including *Charlie Hebdo*, reprint one or more of the cartoons.

- No major U.S. publications reprint the cartoons.

- The U.S. State Department criticizes the publication of the cartoons as "offensive to the beliefs of Muslims." With a perfunctory nod to free speech, the George W. Bush administration goes on to betray that principle by indicating that perhaps the cartoons were better left unpublished.

March 2006: In the United States, the April-May issue of *Free Inquiry* reprints the cartoons, but, citing safety concerns, Borders and Waldenbooks stores refuse to stock that issue of the magazine.

Aftershocks of the Cartoons Crisis

April 2006: Comedy Central refuses to broadcast an image of Muhammad in a *South Park* episode, citing "concerns for public safety."

September 2006: A leading German opera house cancels performances of a Mozart opera, fearing reprisals; the opera includes a scene that depicts the severed head of the prophet Muhammad.

August 2007: For a Swedish exhibition on the theme of the dog in art, the artist Lars Vilks depicts Muhammad as a dog. Because of security fears, organizers of the exhibition rescind Vilks's invitation. An Islamist group in Iraq offers $150,000 bounty for the assassination of Vilks, who is forced to live under police protection.

February 12, 2008: Three Islamists attempt to murder the cartoonist Kurt Westergaard, whose cartoon was one of the twelve originally published by *Jyllands-Posten*. Westergaard was living in hiding under police protection.

March 2008: Osama bin Laden threatens Europeans for repeatedly publishing the Danish cartoons.

June 2008: Exacting revenge for the Danish cartoons, Al Qaeda bombs Denmark's embassy in Pakistan, killing six people.

August 2008: Random House cancels plans to release a novel about the prophet Muhammad's child bride, worried it might "incite acts of violence."

April 2010: Comedy Central receives threats regarding an episode of *South Park* featuring a character claimed to be Muhammad. The network edits the character out of the episode.

April–September 2010: Molly Norris, a cartoonist for *Seattle Weekly*, promotes an "Everybody Draw Muhammad Day" on April 20, 2010. After receiving death threats, she is forced into hiding.

January 1, 2010: Kurt Westergaard escapes another attempt on his life.

May 11, 2011: In Uppsala, Sweden, while giving a talk on freedom of speech, Lars Vilks is attacked.

November 2, 2011: In Paris, France, the offices of the magazine *Charlie Hebdo* are firebombed, following the publication of an edition "guest edited" by Muhammad.

March 1, 2013: In its jihadist recruitment magazine, *Inspire*, Al Qaeda publishes a hit list that includes: Carsten Juste, Flemming Rose, Lars Vilks, Kurt Westergaard, Molly Norris, Stéphane Charbonnier (editor of *Charlie Hebdo*), and Ayaan Hirsi Ali.

November–December 2014: Email servers at Sony Pictures Entertainment are hacked in connection with the release of the comedic film *The Interview*, which is about a plot to assassinate the leader of North Korea.

- Movie theaters are threatened with deadly attacks (the threat warned: "Remember the 11th of September 2001")

- Four national theater chains, which together operate more than 19,000 screens, drop plans to show *The Interview*.

- Citing safety concerns, Sony decides to cancel the theatrical release of *The Interview*.

- Evading the government's fundamental responsibility to protect freedom of speech, President Obama reproaches Sony for failing to stand up for itself.

- Sony reverses its decision, but few theaters agree to screen the movie amid fears of reprisals. The film is released online.

The Massacre at *Charlie Hebdo* and Its Aftershocks

January 7, 2015: In Paris two Islamist gunmen enter the offices of *Charlie Hebdo* and murder twelve people. During the attack they are heard shouting, "We have avenged the Prophet Muhammad" and "God is Great" in Arabic, as they call out the names of the journalists. The gunmen go on to kill a policewoman and four other people during a siege at a kosher supermarket.

January–February 2015:

- Widespread expressions of sympathy for the victims of the attack at *Charlie Hebdo;* #JeSuisCharlie, a hashtag expressing solidarity with the murdered journalists, pervades social media for days.

- On January 11, more than one million people take part in a rally in Paris to remember the victims. Some forty world leaders march in solidarity with France; President Barack Obama is conspicuous by his absence.

- Tide of sympathy recedes; editorials and columns question whether *Charlie Hebdo* brought the massacre upon itself. Calling the journalists at *Charlie Hebdo* "provocateurs," Pope Francis noted that while the massacre was not justified, "a reaction could have been expected."

February 14–15, 2015: In Copenhagen, Denmark, an Islamist gunman opens fire at an event upholding free speech that features Lars Vilks as a speaker. Vilks survives unscathed, but one other is killed.

March–April 2015: PEN American Center, an association of writers and editors, names *Charlie Hebdo* as the winner of the free-speech organization's annual "Freedom of Expression Courage" award. Objecting to the award, six notable authors publicly withdraw from the upcoming PEN gala and award ceremony., More than two hundred members of PEN sign an open letter protesting the decision to honor *Charlie Hebdo*.

April 10, 2015: The cartoonist Garry Trudeau, in a talk accepting a lifetime achievement award, castigates "free speech absolutists." He criticizes not only *Jyllands-Posten* for publishing the cartoons of Muhammad in 2005, but also *Charlie Hebdo* for "punching downward" at a "powerless, disenfranchised minority."

May 3, 2015: In Garland, Texas, two Islamist gunmen open fire outside the Curtis Culwell Center where the "First Annual Muhammad Art Exhibit and Contest" takes place. Police kill both attackers and no innocents are killed.

May–June 2015: Many prominent voices criticize the organizer of the Muhammad art exhibit and contest, Pamela Geller, for "provoking" the Islamist attack.

July 2015: Six months after the massacre at its offices, *Charlie Hebdo* announces that the magazine will stop publishing images of Muhammad.

* * *

Postscript: Iran faced no significant consequences from Western governments for the fatwah against Rushdie. Over the years, the bounty on Rushdie's life has gone up, most recently in February 2016. Currently it stands at nearly $4 million.

* * *

Resources

The above is a selective timeline that omits a great many data points. Comprehensive accounts of the Rushdie affair, the cartoons crisis, and their aftershocks can be found in the following books, which were among the sources used in compiling the timeline:

- *The Rushdie Affair: The Novel, the Ayatollah, and the West* by Daniel Pipes (Transaction Publishers, 2003). Online: amzn.to/1qKY3JL

- *The Tyranny of Silence: How One Cartoon Ignited a Global Debate on the Future of Free Speech* by Flemming Rose (Cato Institute Press, 2014). Online: amzn.to/1VOpFJd

- *Surrender: Appeasing Islam, Sacrificing Freedom* by Bruce Bawer (Random House, 2009). Online: amzn.to/1Sc6Osn

PART 2

Free Speech Fundamentals

Reason requires freedom, self-confidence and self-esteem. It requires the right to think and to act on the guidance of one's thinking—the right to live by one's own independent judgment. Intellectual *freedom cannot exist without political freedom;* political *freedom cannot exist* economic *freedom;* a free mind and a free market are corollaries.

—Ayn Rand, "For the New Intellectual,"
For the New Intellectual

Free Speech Fundamentals

The Nature of Free Speech:
An Interview with Onkar Ghate

The Undercurrent May 19, 2007

*O*nkar Ghate, senior fellow of the Ayn Rand Institute, teaches philosophy at *the Objectivist Academic Center, and lectures on Ayn Rand's ideas across North America. The Undercurrent recently had the pleasure of interviewing him about the Danish cartoon controversy, speech on college campuses, and hate speech.*

The Undercurrent: *Hello Dr. Ghate, and thank you for your time.*

Onkar Ghate: My pleasure. I'm always eager to discuss free speech.

TU: *What is the principle of freedom of speech?*

OG: Freedom of speech is an individual's right to express his ideas without governmental interference, that is, without governmental suppression or censorship.

Freedom of speech is an aspect of the right to liberty. Just as an individual has a right to think for himself and use his mind as he chooses, so he has a right to express the thoughts he has reached in material form, whether orally (in conversation, discussions, lectures, speeches, classes, etc.) or in writing (in books, magazine stories, newspaper articles, web postings, etc.). Freedom of thought is the spiritual aspect of the right to liberty, freedom of speech the material aspect; one represents the mind, the other the body.

The right to free speech, however, is not a right to the material means by which to express one's ideas. These means must be earned. It is not censorship, for example, if a book publisher refuses to publish my book. The owner of a publishing house has the right to decide which views his property will be used to express. If the government were to force him to publish my book (because I have failed to create my own publishing company), the government would be violating the publisher's freedom of speech. The publisher would be forced

63

to express not his own ideas or ideas he thinks should gain a hearing, but ideas with which he disagrees.

Similarly, the right to free speech is not a guarantee of an audience. This too must be earned. Just as I have the right to speak and write what I choose, so other individuals have the right not to listen to or read my views if they so decide. A reader of this paper, for instance, is free to stop reading anytime he chooses.

In essence, freedom of speech is the right to use, without governmental interference, one's own body and property to express ideas to anyone who chooses to listen.

Obviously, an important function of this right is to protect dissenting individuals. Even if everyone else in society regards an individual's ideas as wrong, obnoxious or evil, the government cannot silence him. He remains free to hold and express his views.

TU: *Why is the right to freedom of speech such a crucial value?*

OG: The right to freedom of speech is a crucial value because knowledge is a crucial value. Knowledge is power: it gives one the ability to achieve the goals which further one's life. Think of any profession, from auto mechanic to computer programmer to heart surgeon. What enables members of these professions to rebuild defective engines, to write software to help manage a company's inventory, and to perform open heart surgery? The root of any individual's productive actions is the knowledge he has acquired. But knowledge requires a free mind. A mind can attain knowledge only if it is free to ask questions, free to follow the evidence wherever it leads, free to weigh logically the facts it has discovered. A mind cannot be forced. Knowledge cannot be produced by the barrel of a gun.

A government can suppress an idea, but that does not convince anyone that the idea is false. A government can threaten an individual with fines, imprisonment, even death unless he professes some other idea, but that does not convert the idea into a truth in his mind. Imagine, for a moment, that I was made president of the United States and then tried to spread Ayn Rand's philosophy of reason by physical force (a contradictory pursuit, if ever there was one). Imagine that I threatened citizens with imprisonment unless they professed that rational selfishness is a virtue. Even though I regard this idea as true, my attempt to spread its truth is worse than futile. My threats would create no thought process in the mind of an individual citizen. Indeed, I would paralyze his rational faculty: he would be afraid to think openly about or voice ideas in ethics and would simply parrot slogans he does not understand or accept. This is the nightmare of totalitarian dictatorships, where the minds of millions of starving individuals are destroyed as they are forced to chant, say, that Kim Jong Il is great and communism is the salvation of the masses.

Knowledge—rational understanding—requires a free mind. Such, in essence, is the foundation of an individual's right to freedom of thought and speech.

Now notice an important implication of the freedoms of thought and speech. They necessarily protect a mind that reaches falsehoods, even evil, irrational falsehoods. The right to exercise one's mind necessarily includes the right to choose not to exercise it. Thus in a free society, Nazis, communists and racists, for instance, would have the right to express their vicious irrationalities. If the government were to use the coercive machinery of the state to stop them from voicing their views, the government would become the legislator of "truth." Anyone familiar with the history of the Dark or Middle Ages in Europe or with Galileo's persecution by the Church knows where that leads: to the cessation of thought.

Notice too that an individual uttering the most vicious falsehoods does not infringe on anyone's rights. If someone declared that Asians are morally corrupt (I'm half Indian), he neither "picks my pocket nor breaks my leg," in Thomas Jefferson's memorable words. Such an individual does not interfere with my liberty: I remain free to think, to express my thoughts in material form, and to ignore his falsehoods or oppose them with better ideas if I so choose.

Any actual champion of free speech must therefore possess Voltaire's famous attitude: "I disapprove of what you say, but I will defend to the death your right to say it."

TU: *During the Muhammad cartoon controversy last year, many people argued that banning the cartoons was not a violation of free speech because the cartoons represented hate speech. What is hate speech? Is it an exception to freedom of speech?*

OG: Freedom of speech is a rational principle. Like any rational principle, it is an absolute; which means: within its context it admits of no exceptions.

Apparent exceptions like a man yelling "Fire!" in a crowded movie theater represent a misunderstanding of the principle. As I've said, the principle of freedom of speech states that you can use your own property to express whatever ideas you choose—not that you can use someone else's property. When on another's property, you must abide by the conditions he sets. When you pay to enter a movie theater, for instance, there is an implicit agreement to respect the theater owner's terms of use, which include that you cannot disturb the other customers enjoying the movie by, say, talking on your cell phone during the movie. And you certainly cannot act to recklessly endanger the lives of other customers by, say, pretending there is a fire and creating a riot. An owner of a movie theater could, of course, announce in advance that he allows his customers to say anything they like during the screening of a movie, but likely he wouldn't retain many patrons.

Because freedom of speech is a principle, any "exception" to it actually means its destruction—which brings us to laws against "hate speech."

Such laws seek to ban speech that "offends" or "incites hatred" toward members of a group (the group is usually defined by physiological characteristics like race or gender). Since any idea may "offend" someone or may lead someone to feel hatred toward third parties, what does this amount to in practice? It means that whenever a member of some group finds an idea "offensive" or feels that it will produce hatred against his collective, the government has the power to ban the idea.

This is the death of free speech. By the non-objective standard of "hate speech," any idea can be banned. For instance, to call for the end of the welfare state—as I do—may "offend" a "poverty activist" or may lead people to hate the parasites who choose to live off of productive citizens. So this idea is a candidate for censorship. Or: to claim that the life-giving ideas of the Enlightenment are being subverted and destroyed by many of today's leading intellectuals in the humanities—as I do—may "offend" some university professor or may lead some people to hate these academics. So this idea is a candidate for censorship. Or: the latest breakthrough of a research scientist in genetic engineering may offend an environmentalist or may lead some people to hate those environmentalists who blow up university research laboratories. So the scientist's new idea is a candidate for censorship. Or: an atheist who argues that we should discard belief in God may "offend" a religionist or may cause some people to hate fundamentalist Christians and Muslims. So the atheist's views are candidates for censorship.

The entire sphere of thought, in other words, becomes politicized. What governs now is not the principle of individual liberty but the arbitrary whims of any collective. Under the principle enacted by "hate speech" laws, the individual is no longer free to think and express his thoughts. Instead, he must seek every collective's permission before speaking, making sure that no one is offended by his ideas and that no one takes his ideas as reason to hate anyone or anything.

TU: *Why do you think that many people believe that there is some legitimacy to hate speech laws? Are there deeper philosophical errors that explain the increasing existence and application of such laws?*

OG: One reason is that whenever an individual right begins to be undermined, the attack usually starts with the least attractive exercisers of the right. In the case of the attack on free speech, and especially in the West, among the first victims are individuals who express loathsome ideas, such as support for Nazism and denial of the Holocaust. Many people uncritically think: Would we not be better off without such individuals expressing their evil views? Since, at least sometimes, the immediate result of "hate speech" laws is to ban the views of such individuals, people support the laws without really considering the fundamental principle involved. If they recognized that the cost of silencing such individuals is the destruction of the right to free speech—and that the Government might next censor their ideas—they would think twice. What people must grasp is that the only way to combat irrational ideas is to advocate rational ones—not to reach for the gun of the government.

"Hate speech" laws, however, are not the creation of the public but of academics and intellectuals. The reason such laws are becoming more and more widespread is that Western culture is losing its knowledge of why free speech is a value. As I've indicated, free speech rests on the idea that knowledge is a value and that to be reached, it requires a sovereign, independent mind choosing to exercise its powers of reason. The value of free speech, in other words, rests on a specific view of the human mind.

The dominant voices in the humanities today uphold an opposing view. The human mind, on the modern, anti-Enlightenment approach, is impotent to reach truth; objective human knowledge is a contradiction in terms. On this view, an individual happens to embrace certain ideas because he happens to belong to the white, the black or the Indian race or to the tribe of males, of females, of those born in the West or of those born in the East. Every idea is a prejudice; all that is possible to a human mind is collective subjectivism. The power of reason, on this approach, is a myth.

The end result, logically enough, is to abandon the principle of individual rights. The rights to life, liberty, property and the pursuit of happiness protect the rational mind. They protect the individual's freedom to pursue truth and then to use his newfound knowledge to create the material values that his life and happiness require. But why protect the rational mind, if it cannot reach truth? Throw out reason, in other words, and individual rights lose their meaning.

If reason is discarded, what is left to guide man? His feelings. And so the world becomes a clash of (irreconcilable) prejudices—and every issue is politicized. Why? Because the basic issue in human life now becomes whose whims rule. No dispute has a right and wrong answer. Every dispute is simply a contest to see which group can impose its prejudices by the power of (governmental) force. One group, for instance, wants to express its ideas about terrorism and religion, another group feels that those ideas are "offensive" and "hateful" and should be banned. On the modern approach, there is no objective principle of freedom or individual rights to settle the matter. On the modern approach, the question is simply: whose "feelings" get to rule? And the answer is: the feelings of the collective that is able to seize control of the coercive power of the state. In the present day, this means multiculturalist, feminist, religious and other leaders, who are beginning to succeed in seizing the power of the state, passing "hate speech" laws, and becoming the new thought police.

So I think at a fundamental level, the growing rejection of free speech is caused by the growing rejection of reason. Where there is respect for the power of the individual's rational mind, there is respect for the freedoms of thought and speech; where there is contempt for the power of the individual's rational mind, there is contempt for the freedoms of thought and speech.

TU: *What is hate? Is it ever proper to feel hate toward another individual or group? If so, on what grounds?*

OG: Hatred is an emotion. Broadly speaking, one experiences hatred when one judges that something embodies the antithesis of one's values. Hatred is the opposite of love. As Ayn Rand observed, love is a response to values. One experiences the emotion of love when one judges that something embodies one's values. For instance, one feels love for one's husband or wife, for one's child, for one's friends, for the successful small business one has worked to build up from a fledgling enterprise, and for one's favorite novels and cherished pieces of music which refuel one's spirit. By contrast, one feels hatred for the killer who threatens the life of one's child, for the employee who steals money from one's company, and for the creators of modern "symphonies" of noise, who help destroy the art of music. (Since hatred, like love or any other emotion, is caused by an individual's ideas and judgment, the attempt to ban "hatred" is obviously an attempt to ban ideas.)

Morally, it certainly is appropriate to experience both love and hatred. If one feels love for the good, one will feel hatred for the evil. If one feels love for man's life and the things which further it, one will feel hatred toward that which undermines them. I experience love or hatred toward many things—and regard both of these emotions as appropriate. Just as I love creators like Thomas Edison, so I hate destroyers like Hitler. Just as I love freedom fighters like Thomas Jefferson, so I hate the religionists who flew planes into the World Trade Center. Just as I love Ayn Rand's philosophy of Objectivism, so I hate the ideologies of communism and socialism. I regard these experiences of hatred as appropriate because the emotions flow from what I think are correct ideas and evaluations: the things I hate are, in one form or another, inimical to man's life. (Though evil must be opposed and combated, it and the emotions it engenders should never be granted the importance one grants to the good. One should never become consumed by hatred.)

Of course in a moral context hatred is appropriate only in regard to that which is open to an individual's choice. It is appropriate to feel hatred toward Osama bin Laden for the murderous actions he chose to perform. It is inappropriate to feel hatred toward a black for the color of his skin or a male for the gender of his body. It can be appropriate to feel hatred toward a group of individuals, but only when membership in the group is a product of choice. It is appropriate to feel hatred toward the Nazi leadership taken as a whole, because the various individuals chose to join the party and give their support to Hitler. It is inappropriate to feel hatred towards blacks or males as a group.

So one judges an emotion by the rationality or irrationality of the ideas which generate it. This is why one judges the emotions of hatred of a racist as morally monstrous. To believe that the content of a person's mind and character is determined by his unchosen "membership" in a physiological group—as racists do believe—is irrational. But to legally punish a racist for feeling hatred is precisely to punish him for the ideas he holds. To do so is to violate his freedom of thought. (It is of course a radically different issue if a racist takes physical action to violate another individual's rights; but even here, the racist should be punished for his action, not for his hatred.)

TU: *What, if anything, can students do to promote freedom of speech on university campuses? What role does Ayn Rand's philosophy of Objectivism play in the struggle to maintain free speech in America?*

OG: To promote freedom of speech, students must understand its nature. In my estimation, this requires studying the works of Ayn Rand. She is the most penetrating and principled defender of individual rights.

Observe that mysticism and blind faith lead, politically, to authoritarianism—as the West witnessed for centuries after the fall of Rome. In that kind of culture, liberty is non-existent. Observe also that skepticism and the rule of whim lead, politically, to gang warfare—as the West is now witnessing as group after group seeks the political power to ban that which it considers "offensive." In this kind of culture too, liberty disappears. Only a defense of reason can provide the foundation for a defense of the rights to freedom of thought and speech.

And this makes Ayn Rand's philosophy indispensable in the battle for free speech. Taking a historical perspective, Ayn Rand's accomplishment in my view is that she completed the defense of reason that Aristotle began. Aristotle defended the power of the rational mind against both the mysticism of Plato and the skepticism of the Sophists. Ayn Rand's philosophic achievement is to defend the power of the rational mind against today's hordes of Kantian-inspired mystics and skeptics. (For the details, one must of course study her works.)

Equipped with the knowledge that Ayn Rand uniquely provides, students would be able to argue effectively for free speech and against the imposition of public university speech codes, the banning of speakers from campuses, "hate speech" laws, etc. Faced with a principled opposition—one able to articulate the connection between reason and freedom of speech—university administrations and, more widely, the culture may reconsider the issue. (Remember, however, that a private university has the right to impose speech codes and ban speakers, no matter how irrational its grounds for doing so.) The battle for liberty is an intellectual battle. It can be won only with the proper intellectual ammunition.

Thought Control

Onkar Ghate April 22, 2003

You are jolted awake at 1:00 a.m. by loud knocking on the door. Alarmed, you and your girlfriend rise to answer. The police barge in and arrest you both on suspicion of having had premarital sex. Sound like something that would happen only in a dictatorship like Iraq or China? Next week the U.S. Supreme Court will hear a case that if not overturned will grant legitimacy to such governmental power. (In a disturbing 1986 decision the Court upheld the constitutionality of such power.)

The case is *Lawrence v. Texas*. In 1998 Texas police, responding to a neighbor's deliberately false report of an armed intruder in the apartment of John Geddes Lawrence, entered his unlocked apartment. Discovering that Lawrence and Tyron Garner were having consensual sex, the police jailed them on charges of violating Texas's Homosexual Conduct Law. Lawrence and Garner are now challenging the law.

At issue is not whether a particular sexual practice among consenting adults is in fact moral or immoral. At issue is something much broader: whether the government should have the power to enter your home and arrest you for having sex because it regards your sexual desires as "base," the power to enter your laboratory and arrest you for running a scientific experiment because it regards your research as "sinful," or the power to enter your business and arrest you for making money because it regards the profit motive as "wicked."

At issue is whether the government should have the power to legislate morality.

If you want to live in a free society, the answer is: No.

To answer "No" does not mean we should throw out laws punishing murder. It means the government's function is not to become the thought police, charged with ensuring that citizens act on correct ideas. The government's function is only to stop an individual from taking action (e.g., murder) that violates the rights of other individuals. It means that the absolute moral principles at the foundation of a free society preclude the government from becoming policeman of morality.

Our Founding Fathers understood that, like any other form of knowledge, moral knowledge—knowledge of good and evil—requires a mind free to follow the observed facts and evidence wherever they lead. They therefore created a political system that protects the sovereignty of the rational mind—the very source of rights. Each American has the right to think, to express his thoughts in conversations, speeches and books, and then to act on his thought in pursuit of the values his life and happiness require. (So long, of course, as he respects the same rights of others.) He must have these freedoms because knowledge comes not from obedience to authority but from reason. "Fix reason firmly in her seat," Jefferson explained to his nephew, "and call on her tribunal for every fact, every opinion. Question with boldness even the existence of a God; because, if there be one, he must more approve of the homage of reason than that of blindfolded fear."

To incarcerate John Lawrence because he engaged in homosexual sex is to do violence to his reason.

According to Lawrence's judgment, sex with the right, consenting adult represents an important, moral, life-affirming pleasure. The state demands that he discard this judgment—or face jail. But to force someone to obey produces no moral enlightenment in his mind; it only incapacitates his means of understanding. Even granting for the sake of argument only that homosexuality is immoral, in jailing Lawrence and Garner the government does not persuade them that their action is wrong. It merely makes them fear believing and acting on what they continue to think is right. No knowledge, moral or otherwise, can be implanted by the instruments of coercion. "Force and mind," in Ayn Rand's memorable words, "are opposites; morality ends where a gun begins."

Observe that the need of a mind to be free in order to reach knowledge implies that it has the right to make mistakes (you may think Lawrence and Garner mistaken). There is no such thing as the freedom to think so long as you reach "government approved" ideas. That would make the state guardian of "truth." That road leads only to what it always has led to: the non-thought of, say, the Taliban's Afghanistan, Soviet Russia or Europe's Dark Ages.

In essence the government of a free society bans only one action—the initiation of physical force—precisely because force prevents an individual from following the judgment of his mind. The government of a free society does not seek to control its citizens' thoughts by, say, jailing homosexuals or hypocrites. Its function is to stop other people from violating one's rights, not to force them to be good—which is a contradiction in terms.

Force vs. mind, authority vs. reason, obedience vs. thought—that is what is at issue in *Lawrence v. Texas*. At the birth of this great nation Jefferson swore "eternal hostility against every form of tyranny over the mind of man." Let us hope today's Supreme Court remembers his words. Otherwise, the government's next knock on the door may be for me or you.

At the Heart of the Attacks on Free Speech, an Attack on Reason

Steve Simpson   December 21, 2015

In his terrific book *The Tyranny of Silence*, Flemming Rose, who was at the center of the Danish cartoons crisis in 2005–06, quotes Saudi cleric and TV preacher Muhammad Al-Munajjid's reaction to the controversy: "The problem is that they want to open a debate on whether Islam is true or not . . . . they want to open up everything for a debate. That's it. It begins with freedom of thought, it continues with freedom of speech, and it ends up with freedom of belief."

Keep that quote in mind as you consider a December 2015 article in *The New Yorker* titled "The Hit List," which reports that Islamists have been systematically murdering atheist bloggers in Bangladesh since 2013. The article is a chilling reminder that Islamists agree with Al-Munajjid's disdain for free thought and free speech and that they are willing to express that disdain by killing those who question their religion. We've seen this view at work many times before, of course—in the fatwah against Salman Rushdie, in the Danish cartoons controversy and ensuing death threats against the cartoonists and publishers, in the attacks on *Charlie Hebdo* and Pamela Geller's Muhammad cartoon contest in Garland, Texas. This time, the attacks are against atheist bloggers in Bangladesh who have the temerity to question religion (not just Islam, mind you. *All* religion).

Note that these bloggers are not "provocateurs" in the sense in which many intellectuals criticized *Charlie Hebdo* and Pamela Geller after the attacks on them. Although some of the bloggers' commentary is biting and satirical, no one could accuse them of engaging in ridicule for the sake of ridicule. (For the record, I don't think that charge is accurate for any of the Muhammad cartoonists or publishers, either, and even if it were, it wouldn't justify the attacks and threats against them.) Nor are the bloggers "powerful" Westerners "punching downward" at a "disenfranchised minority" as Garry Trudeau and many others claimed of *Charlie Hebdo*. Quite the contrary. The Bangladeshi bloggers are a small minority of atheists who are questioning and criticizing religion. Unfortunately for them, the dominant religion in their country is Islam, and the bloggers are living in a time and place in which a significant number of Islam's followers believe that heretics deserve death.

That is the reason Islamists regularly murder those who disagree with them. They take very seriously an ideology that rejects reality and reason in favor of mysticism and revelation. The true and the good are beyond our comprehension, according to Islam (and all religions). Knowledge is handed down to us by Allah or God or Yahweh, interpreted by His chosen representatives on earth (priests and imams) and disseminated in the form of commandments written in sacred texts. If I may torture a line from "The Charge of the Light Brigade," ours is not to reason why, ours is just to do or die.

Attacks on thought and dissent by Islamists have nothing to do with alleged "oppression" by the West or the particular form that criticism of their religion takes. It has everything to do with a mystical ideology that mandates death for unbelievers. Anyone who takes that ideology seriously and is committed to following it will come to the same conclusion as the cleric Flemming Rose quoted in his book. It isn't just particularly inflammatory commentary they oppose. They cannot abide *any* critical analysis of their religion, because that will naturally lead people to question the entire structure of an ideology that cannot hold up to rational scrutiny. What they oppose isn't just offensive speech or even free speech as such. They oppose the root of free speech, which is free thought.

Unfortunately, Islamists aren't the only ones who fundamentally oppose free thought and free speech. On this point, they have intellectual allies in the West, particularly among postmodern intellectuals and their fellow travelers. Consider the following quote:

> [A]bstract concepts like free speech do not have any "natural" content but are filled with whatever content and direction one can manage to put into them. "Free speech" is just the name we give to **verbal behavior** that serves the substantive agendas we wish to advance; and we give our preferred verbal behaviors that name when we can, when we have the **power** to do so . . . . **Free speech, in short, is not an independent value but a political prize, and if that prize has been captured by a politics opposed to yours, it can no longer be invoked in ways that further your purposes, for it is now an obstacle to those purposes.**

That's postmodernist Stanley Fish from an essay appropriately titled "There's No Such Thing as Free Speech, and It's a Good Thing, Too." (The bolding in the quote is mine). Certainly, Fish is not calling for an attack on those who disagree with him. But he is attacking our very means of agreement or disagreement: our minds. Postmodernists hold that reason, objectivity, and the very idea of free speech and persuasion are illusions. They are all tools of oppression that the "powerful" use to impose their views on the "powerless," typically through institutions like law and government.

You can find a lot of thinkers today who share this basic view of reason and objectivity and who therefore view Western civilization, especially America, as an oppressive society with racism, sexism, classism and every other sort of "ism" built right into the fabric of the ideas on which our civilization is based. They don't all call themselves postmodernists, but their approach is very "postmodern" in that they oppose the Enlightenment ideas of reason, free will, political freedom, capitalism, industrialization, and the pursuit of happiness. These are the ideas that spawned the modern era.

Postmodern intellectuals attack these ideas at their root by attacking reason, objectivity and the very existence of a reality outside ourselves. (Many are social subjectivists, meaning they believe that reality is essentially created by society, typically through the operation of language.) As a result, they view law and government as inherently subjective institutions incapable of serving universal principles based on objective facts. According to postmodernists, these institutions are not used to protect, but to oppress.

You can see that basic view in Stanley Fish's comment, above. Or consider the highly influential French postmodernist Michel Foucault, who believed that it is "meaningless to speak in the name of— or against—Reason, Truth, or Knowledge." "Reason," according to Foucault, "is the ultimate language of madness." According to another postmodernist, "[r]eason and power are one and the same."

If you take these ideas seriously, it is natural to conclude, as Fish does, that free speech is a cruel joke played on the hapless masses who do not know they are being deceived into submitting to the will of a powerful elite that is oppressing them. It also follows that trying to convince people to change their views about social institutions is pointless. As postmodernist Frank Lentricchia has said, his philosophy "seeks not to find the foundation and the conditions of truth but to exercise power for the purpose of social change." Postmodernists therefore attempt to guide students to "spot, confront, and work against the political horrors of one's time." (Several of my references and quotes here come from Professor Stephen Hicks's book *Explaining Postmodernism*.)

That is, in essence, what Herbert Marcuse, widely known as the philosopher of the New Left during the 1960s, taught his students—which included many of today's college professors. Marcuse is one of the first mainstream thinkers (at least in the West) to attack freedom of speech openly, which he did in a 1965 essay called "Repressive Tolerance." Because Western civilization is inherently oppressive, according to Marcuse, speech should be free for those who oppose freedom, capitalism and the foundations of Western society, but not for those who defend them.

To see the consequences of these ideas, look at what is happening on the postmodernist playgrounds that our institutions of higher learning have become. Students regularly occupy administrative offices and issue lists of demands, they physically bar journalists from observing their public protests (free speech for me, but not for thee!), they disrupt debates and oppose commencement speakers, they call for "safe spaces" to protect them from disagreeable ideas, and they often demand censorship of those ideas. Oppression, inequality, and systemic racism and sexism are the constant refrains used to justify these actions, whether there is evidence to support these claims or not.

Or consider the appeasing attitude among so many Western intellectuals today toward terrorism, in which the terrorists' actions are explained away and the victims are blamed for "provoking" them. Witness Garry Trudeau's criticisms of *Charlie Hebdo* and the PEN award controversy, in which over two hundred authors angrily denounced the organization when it presented *Charlie Hebdo* with an award for courage. Witness the many people, including the *New York Times* editorial board, who criticized Pamela Geller for "provoking" the Garland attacks. Witness New York *Daily News* columnist Linda Stasi's execrable op-ed after the San Bernardino shooting, which lumped one of the victims in with the terrorists on the grounds that they were all "haters" (thus ignoring the difference between expressing one's ideas with speech and doing so with bullets). Witness the constant use of the term "Islamophobia," which equates criticism of Islam and its practitioners with an irrational psychological condition.

Fundamentally, what postmodern intellectuals and those they have influenced have in common is an opposition to (and often hatred of) reason. Reality, they argue, is beyond our comprehension and is instead a manifestation of our subjective desires. (Marcuse believed that the ideal society is one in which people have an essentially effortless existence.) Western institutions like freedom, the rule of law, and capitalism, therefore, are mere social constructs. Because they lead to oppression, inequality, and poverty, it's time to construct them differently. As Marcuse summed up his view: "The logic of thought is slavery. Capitalism is freedom which is slavery plus technology. Freedom is a concentration camp. Freedom is slavery." Not exactly tantalizing prose, but the point is hard to miss.

Americans have been weaned on these ideas since at least the 1960s. Is it any wonder that polls show waning support for free speech? That when terrorists attack us, many of our leading intellectuals express sympathy for them (they are poor and disenfranchised, they feel powerless, they feel oppressed, Israel is bullying them, America has taken all their oil, etc.) or chide anyone who offends them for "provoking" the attacks?

Postmodernists and their fellow travelers don't come to their views in precisely the same way as Islamists, but the two groups end up in the same place, intellectually speaking. Islamists believe that reality is an illusion created for us by an all-powerful entity called "Allah." Postmodernists and other prominent intellectuals believe that reality is an illusion created for us by an all-powerful entity called "the State" or "society." Both pine for an effortless existence (in heaven or at the expense of the rich and powerful who stole this existence from the poor and oppressed). Both believe that the average man cannot understand the world or how to act in it and therefore needs an intellectual elite to tell him what to do. For Islamists, it's imams. For secularists, it's Cass Sunstein and other "czars" who will "nudge" us to do the right things.

Certainly, Western intellectuals are not advocating violence. But it's worth recognizing that when a nudge doesn't work, a good swift kick is sure to follow. As Ayn Rand said in her essay "Faith and Force: The Destroyers of the Modern World": "Anyone who resorts to the formula: 'It's so, because I say so,' will have to reach for a gun sooner or later." That is true whether the particular faith at issue is religious or secular. And while the secular proponents are not reaching for guns (yet), note that their college protégés seem to be inching ever closer to that point, and there is no shortage of calls for censorship among intellectuals these days.

Defending free speech takes more than the argument that speech doesn't hurt anyone. To defend freedom of any variety requires defending reason and the other Enlightenment ideas as positive and irreplaceable values of human life. It also requires us to reject and condemn irrational ideas from any quarter. Ayn Rand did that. Look to Bangladesh, the Middle East, Europe, and America's campuses for a vision of what happens, ultimately, if the rest of us don't.

Campus Speech Controversies

Steve Simpson November 25, 2015

Anyone who has been paying attention to college campuses in recent weeks knows that something seems to have changed in the way today's students think. At the University of Missouri, students who staged a protest over alleged racism on campus physically blocked student journalists from taking photographs and videotaping the event. Their reason? They wanted to create their own "narrative" and keep media from invading their "safe space." When one student refused to stop videotaping the event, a professor who was helping the protesters called for "some muscle" to have him removed. Keep in mind that this was a public protest on university property. Later, at Yale, students flew into a rage when a professor took issue with an administration email admonishing students not to wear Halloween costumes that might offend others. She argued that students were mature enough to deal with potentially offensive situations and suggested that they try talking to one another to resolve their concerns and differences. As if to prove her positive view of students wrong, a group of them quickly called for her removal and trotted out the now familiar complaint that her views made them feel "unsafe."

Similar things have been happening at colleges across the nation for years. Students demand trigger warnings and "safe spaces" to protect them from controversial ideas. They see racism, sexism, "homophobia," and a host of "microaggressions" in seemingly innocuous and often true statements. (The University of California school system published a list of microagressions that includes phrases such as "America is the land of opportunity" and "I believe the most qualified person should get the job" among the transgressions). Students occupy university offices and publish lists of demands, which typically include more "diversity," sensitivity training for professors and students, and, of course, speech codes.

What is going on?

Ayn Rand addresses an earlier manifestation of the same phenomenon in a series of essays about the student protests of the 1960s and the New Left that was emerging at the time. They are collected in *Return of the Primitive: The Anti-Industrial Revolution* (which was originally published as *The New Left: The Anti-Industrial Revolution*). Rand's views are just as relevant today as they were then. Indeed, they are perhaps more important to understand now because today we are seeing the consequences that she warned of over forty years ago.

In my view, the best essay for gaining an overall understanding of what is happening on America's campuses right now is "The Cashing-In: The Student 'Rebellion.'" Rand analyses the student rebellion that started on Berkeley's campus in the mid-1960s and the so-called Free Speech Movement that went along with it, the philosophical character of the movement, its goals and why it started. The title hints at her explanation of this latter point: what the students were "cashing in" on were the dominant trends in philosophy—"epistemological agnosticism, avowed irrationalism, ethical subjectivism"—which they were absorbing in the very schools against which they were rebelling. One can see these same ideas at the core of today's student radicals, although it is becoming a bit clearer where they lead.

The clarity of consequences and thus goals of a philosophical movement is the subject of another essay in the book, "The Left: Old and New," in which Rand compares the New Left campus radicals of the 1960s with the old leftists of the 1930s and '40s. She pronounces the old left "cleaner" in the sense that they at least gave a nod to the importance of science and industrialization even while they preached collectivism and supported dictatorial regimes like the Soviet Union. But because collectivism is incompatible with individual initiative and thought, which is the source of science and the values it yields, the new leftists of the 1960s jettisoned any pretense toward industrialization and technology in favor of nature and the noble (noble-sounding, at least) savagery of the hippies. As Rand observes, "Confronted with the choice of an industrial civilization or collectivism, it is an industrial civilization that the liberals discarded. Confronted with the choice of technology or dictatorship, it is technology that they discarded. Confronted with the choice of reason or whims, it is reason that they discarded." Through the many incarnations of the left in this country, the three fundamentals that have remained untouched, explains Rand, are: "mysticism-altruism-collectivism" and their "psychological manifestation: the lust for power; i.e., the lust to destroy."

Do Rand's insights hold up today? Consider the actions of today's campus protesters and especially how quickly most thinkers on the left have given up on freedom of speech as a principle, which, for most of my lifetime, many liberals championed courageously.

Lest you think that college is the only place students can absorb bad ideas, keep in mind that the students who are whining about offensive Halloween costumes and demanding "safe spaces" had to have learned *something* before they arrived at college. In "The Comprachicos," Rand evaluates the source of that something—progressive education—and pronounces it destructive. The title of the article refers to groups Victor Hugo describes in his novel *The Man Who Laughs* that mutilate children to turn them into circus freaks. Rand uses the metaphor as a segue into a critique of modern teaching methods that destroy, not children's bodies, but their minds by hobbling their ability to think. The essay was the first thing that came to mind when I watched the now famous video from the Yale Halloween controversy showing a young woman screeching at a professor over the incident. Throughout the video, the woman demands that Yale be turned into a "safe space." Safe from what, you might ask? Ideas is one answer. Life is probably a better one.

Of course, because the free speech controversies on campus are so wrapped up in claims of widespread racism, be sure to read "Racism," Rand's clarifying essay on the subject as well. Unlike many of today's intellectuals and the young people they influence, Rand understands racism to be "the lowest, most crudely primitive form of collectivism." It is "the caveman's version of the doctrine of innate ideas—or of inherited knowledge—which has been thoroughly refuted by philosophy and science. Racism is a doctrine of, by and for brutes." Certainly, racist laws and government policies have no place in a free society. But the solution to racism, whether past or present, as Rand argues, is not race-based laws or the hyper-race consciousness we see all around us today. It is freedom and respect for the individual. "The smallest minority on earth," Rand once noted, "is the individual." Treat individuals as ends in themselves and protect their rights to do and think as they please and the sort of widespread racism we have seen in the past will ultimately die a natural death.

Finally, if you want a sense of why college administrators and professors constantly cave to the demands of the protesters and other agitators on campuses today, I would recommend reading Rand's essay "Altruism as Appeasement" in *The Voice of Reason: Essays in Objectivist Thought*.

At their core, today's student protests, like yesterday's, are motivated by evil ideas, most notably mysticism, altruism, and collectivism. The solution, as Rand repeatedly argues in many contexts, is to replace those ideas with the ideas that are fundamentally consistent with reality and man's nature—reason, egoism, and individualism.

Free Speech on Campus

Onkar Ghate   February 11, 2005

Because the comments Professor Ward Churchill made shortly after September 11 have come to light—obscene comments in which he vilifies the World Trade Center victims as "little Eichmanns" and lauds their killers as "humanitarians"—Churchill has resigned as chairman of the University of Colorado's ethnic studies department. But, with the support of other faculty, he retains his professorship. Four members of his department have expressed "unconditional support" for his "freedom of expression and First Amendment rights." The Faculty Assembly of the university, though it regards his words as "controversial, offensive, and odious," defends his freedom to utter them.

In opposition, Colorado Gov. Bill Owens has called for Churchill's resignation, saying that taxpayers should not have to subsidize Churchill's "outrageous and insupportable" views.

Both solutions are incompatible with free speech.

Freedom of speech is an individual's right to express ideas without coercive interference from the government. Free speech does protect an individual who voices unpopular ideas from governmental force, but it does not require that other citizens support him. If an individual wants others to finance the expression of his ideas, he must seek their voluntary agreement. To force another person to support ideas he opposes violates his freedom of speech.

A journalist, for instance, has the freedom to write what he pleases, but he has no right to demand that *Time* magazine publish it. That decision belongs to the owners of *Time*. Similarly, a professor has the freedom to teach any view he wishes, but he has no right to demand that Harvard employ him. That decision belongs to the private owners of Harvard. Freedom of speech is not the right of a Ph.D. to have other citizens provide him with a university classroom.

Yet that in effect is what the professors are demanding.

They maintain that no matter how much the citizens who fund public universities may disagree with a professor's views, he should be able to continue to exist on the public dole. Taxpayers are to be stripped of their right to choose which ideas their money supports. Why? So that professors can spout whatever theories happen to catch their fancy—including those that brand productive Americans as Nazis and Islamic

83

killers as liberators—without the burden of having to seek the voluntary consent of those forced to sponsor them.

Under the guise of defending free speech, therefore, the professors are actually advocating its destruction.

But it is no solution for the government to put pressure (or worse) on public universities whenever a professor teaches ideas opposed to the views of a majority of taxpayers. The moment the government becomes arbiter of what can and cannot be taught on campus, the moment speech becomes subject to majority vote, censorship results.

What then is the answer? Privatize the universities.

The truth is that public education as such is antithetical to free speech. Whether leftists are forced to pay taxes to fund universities from which their academic spokesmen are barred (as Gov. Owens's solution requires), or non-leftists are forced to pay taxes to fund professors who condemn America as a terrorist nation, someone loses the right to choose which ideas his money supports.

By its nature, a public university must make decisions about what to include in and to exclude from its curriculum. Of necessity, therefore, some citizens will object to what is being taught in its classrooms. But they are nevertheless forced to finance the communication of those ideas.

To safeguard the right to freedom of speech, the right to private property must be safeguarded. Only private universities can protect free speech. The owners of a university could then hire the faculty they endorsed, while others could refuse to fund the university if they disagreed with its teachings.

However, since privatization would threaten the left's grip on the universities—as well as any professor who enjoys the unearned privilege of spewing out ideas without worrying about the need to finance their expression—many professors vehemently oppose this solution. In the name of free speech, they denounce as "tyranny of the almighty dollar" the sole means of preserving free speech.

But we must not be fooled by this cry from the professors about their freedom of speech. Freedom is precisely what they don't advocate. We are right in objecting to being forced to fund their ideas, loathsome or otherwise. The only solution, however, is a free market in education.

Free Speech, Politics, and the Trump Controversy: An Interview with Steve Simpson

The Undercurrent March 25, 2016

Steve Simpson is the director of Legal Studies at the Ayn Rand Institute. A former constitutional litigator for the Institute for Justice, Simpson has litigated major constitutional cases in courts across the nation, including the United States Supreme Court. Simpson writes and speaks on a wide variety of legal and constitutional issues, including free speech and campaign finance law, cronyism and government corruption, and the rule of law. The rise of Donald Trump and recent violence at his rallies have prompted much discussion about free speech issues, in politics and more broadly. The Undercurrent's J. A. Windham had the pleasure of speaking with Simpson on these timely issues.

The Undercurrent: *There's been a lot of discussion lately about free speech on the campaign trail—when it applies, who supports it, etc. I'd like to kick us off with a basic question: What is "free speech," and why should we care about it?*

Steve Simpson: "Free speech" is the term we use for the legal right to engage in speech protected by the Constitution, but also the individual *moral* right to speak freely. And the proper meaning of that right—to boil it down to its essence—is that it protects your freedom to say what you want, about anything you want, so long as you don't use speech to violate the rights of others (which is true of any right). So, for example, you don't have the right to commit fraud or libel, to threaten others, or to incite violence.

The core of the right—why we have it to begin with—is that we're thinking beings who have to use our minds to guide our actions. One way we do that is by communicating with other people. We live in society, which is a huge benefit, and we therefore should and must have the right not only to think for ourselves but to express our thoughts to other people.

As long as you do that in a way that respects the rights of others, the proper understanding of the right to free speech is that you can say *any damn thing you want*. Now, that's not how it's understood today, and

---

This interview originally appeared on the website of The Undercurrent (theundercurrent.org).

there's a lot of confusion about what the right entails. We've seen that a lot in recent times with popular objections to "offensive" speech and calls to limit political speech, but views like these ultimately flow from an improper understanding of the right to free speech.

TU: *How do you view the relationship between freedom of speech and political discourse in this country? What role does the First Amendment play in this relationship?*

SS: Let me address a preliminary issue first. We need to ask ourselves: "What is the relationship between freedom of speech and civilized society?" Political discourse is obviously part of civilized society and is very important, but the importance of free speech goes far beyond that. I would call free speech one of the *foundations* of civilized society. Simply put, you can't have a free society like ours without protections for freedom of speech.

Ayn Rand once said that the two primary benefits we get from civilized society are the division of labor (specialization, trade, and cooperation) and the accumulation and dissemination of knowledge. Progress happens in a society only because people can profit from the knowledge and ingenuity of others through communication and trade. None of that can happen without freedom of speech. So one way to think about the importance of free speech is that, without it, you don't get the modern world and all of its amazing benefits.

Now, with that context in mind, it's easy to see how important free speech is to politics. We really couldn't have the type of government the Founders gave us—a government that protects our rights—without freedom of speech. In fact, one of the reasons they included the First Amendment in the Constitution was to protect the right to speak about government. This is one of the reasons campaign finance laws are such a flagrant violation of the First Amendment. In essence, they seek to limit and ration people's speech on an issue that is vitally important, which is politics.

You can actually see a lot of what I've said about free thought and free speech reflected in the First Amendment itself. The structure of the Amendment is really quite fascinating. It starts with the freedom of religion clauses, then it goes to free speech, then freedom of the press, assembly, and petition. And if you think about it, there's a logical order to that: first is freedom of conscience (which you can think of as free thought on the type of fundamental questions that religion involves), and then it goes to the various expressions of that principle—first to speech, then to the main means of mass communication at the time, which was the press, then to the right to associate and speak out with others (freedom of assembly), and finally to the right to speak directly to government, which is the right to petition.

This circles back to something that I raised before, which is that the core of the right to free speech is freedom of thought, which goes to the role of reason in human life. We have to guide our own lives, we have to make choices, and we have to think to survive. In order to do that, we have to be free—both to think and to act on our thoughts, and therefore to communicate with others. That's not just because it's fun to talk to other people, but because part of the process of figuring out what's true and good in our lives involves discussion and debate. Think about it from the perspective of the scientific method. You put your data and your ideas out there, others evaluate and possibly criticize them, and through the process of deliberation and debate, trial and error, everyone learns. Freedom of speech—indeed, freedom in general—is absolutely essential to this process.

TU: *I'd like to apply some of this to recent events. For instance, much has been made of the so-called riots that prompted the cancellation of a Donald Trump campaign rally in Chicago last week, which Trump and many others have described as a violation of his First Amendment rights. Are they right?*

SS: No. Those aren't violations of the First Amendment, but they could still be violations of his and other people's rights. The First Amendment is a restriction on government and government *only*. What it essentially says is that government can't make any laws that abridge your freedom of speech. It doesn't apply to private parties at all. But to be clear, that doesn't mean protesters can disrupt a Trump rally or prevent him or others from speaking—or, for that matter, that Trump supporters can prevent others from speaking. It just means that the conduct of private parties toward one another is a matter for criminal and tort law to resolve, not the First Amendment.

So while protesters blocking your way to a Trump rally (as we saw last week) is not a violation of the First Amendment, it's still *criminal conduct*—it's a violation of your personal right to go where you want, to own and use property, to trade and deal with others, etc. This is precisely why we criminalize conduct like assault, battery, trespass, and the like. And from that standpoint, there's bad conduct on *both* sides of this dispute.

It may be helpful to recall what I said earlier about the nature of rights, which is that they protect your freedom of action, but only to the extent that you don't infringe the rights of others. One way to think about rights is that they define zones of freedom within which you have the authority to act to carry on your life. They exist to *prevent* conflicts, not to create them.

One of the great confusions about free speech today is that it's somehow a "special" right that trumps other rights. A common example of this is the idea that my right to speak somehow trumps your property rights, so that protesters have the right to invade a private gathering and disrupt the speakers. That's completely wrong. I have the right to free speech—on *my* property, and at *my* expense. I don't have the right to come into your living room and deliver a political lecture to you. And if I did, you would have every right to tell me to leave. That's not a violation of my right to free speech; it's an example of you invoking your right to your own property.

This apparent "clash" of rights is where I think a lot of confusion about free speech comes from. The Supreme Court has held that you have the right to speak in a public space or on a street corner so long as you don't disrupt other people's right to travel and carry on their lives. But people often times confuse that with the idea that they therefore have the right to speak anywhere they want. Assuming Trump's rallies are private and he paid for the venue, he can tell you to shut up or leave. Now, we might criticize him for that, depending on the circumstances. But that's no violation of your right to free speech. You don't have a right to go into somebody else's arena and blabber on while they're giving a speech.

TU: *Let's talk about what happens in those arenas. Recently, increasing violence at Trump's rallies, coupled with comments that appear to show the candidate at least encouraging physical confrontation, have led some to accuse him of "inciting violence" and others to defend the encouragement as protected free speech. Can you tell us a bit about what "incitement" actually is, and whether Trump is really committing it? If not, is he engaged in protected speech?*

SS: Sure. Let's start with what the crime is, and we'll go from there. "Incitement," simply put, is calling on people to engage in violence or unlawful behavior. It can get complicated, but to understand it, it's helpful to know that in the criminal law, there are all sorts of ways to violate other people's rights and to break the law by acting in concert with others. For example, you could pay someone else to hurt or kill another person or to steal his property, or you could concoct a plan for a number of people to achieve those ends together. There are a number of categories in the criminal law that cover conduct like this, such as aiding and abetting, solicitation, and conspiracy. Incitement is in the same type of category—it's a kind of collective lawlessness. It's one person encouraging another, and both of them, in a sense, joining together to commit some violation of rights or the law. The classic example of incitement is that you're in a crowd of people who are restless or angry and verging on violence, and you say something like "let's all get together and loot that store." You're as guilty as they are for the ultimate robbery because you intended to bring it about, and you would be properly subject to criminal punishment for that.

Based on what I've read, it sounds like Trump may have committed incitement on a couple of occasions during his rallies, when he has said things that seem like they are encouraging his supporters to use force and violence against protesters. But to really judge that accurately would take more than just reading a few news reports.

TU: *So how should the attendees at Trump rallies or Trump himself respond to these protesters?*

SS: Assuming Trump has the exclusive right to use the venue, then the answer is either don't let them in, or, if they get in and you can't convince them to stop, call the police. As far as I can tell, the people who are coming in and protesting Trump rallies are trespassing and physically impeding other people from engaging in conduct—holding a rally and speaking or listening—that Trump's supporters have every right to engage in.

But the fact that somebody trespasses on your property doesn't give you the right to right to punch him or tackle him and drag him bodily out the door. The proper response is to call the police and let them take care of that. Of course, you have the right to defend yourself to the extent that it's necessary to prevent someone from harming you. But short of that, call the police.

TU: *In another vein, Trump has expressed a desire to "open up our libel laws" so that he can sue media outlets that criticize him. What do you make of this proposal?*

SS: I make of it that it's completely stupid. And I put it that way on purpose, because it's a totally unserious proposal that betrays a real ignorance of law and government, not to mention a real disdain for free speech. The president doesn't have the power to change the libel laws. He'd have to change the law in all fifty states and then overturn a lot of Supreme Court precedent or amend the Constitution. His view on this (and many other things) is cause for concern because he's *running for president*—he's going to have a lot of power over other people. So even though he can't just up and change the libel laws, it's troubling that somebody with that kind of authority would boast about his intent to use the power of the presidency against people who criticize him.

Political candidates willingly put themselves in a position in which they're obviously going to be criticized and in which they *should* be criticized. I wouldn't go as far as to say that they should never be able to sue for libel, but if you're going to run for an office that gives you the kind of power politicians wield today, the law should give ample leeway to allow people to criticize you (and I think the Supreme Court has done a pretty good job of establishing the right standards). I usually find it tiresome for any politician to whine about the media being "unfair" or the like, but for a candidate to threaten to use the power of law against the media is scary.

TU: *What's your ultimate assessment of Donald Trump on freedom of speech: friend or foe?*

SS: I would put it like this: Trump, like most candidates for political office today, is not a friend of *freedom* itself. The issue is not just about free speech, which he seems not to understand or care about at all. Trump is anti-intellectual and opposed to freedom at its core.

To take one example, after the attacks on the "Draw Muhammad" contest in Garland, Texas, Trump's reaction was something like "Don't you have anything else to draw? Why are you drawing pictures of Muhammad? Draw something else." Not only does this ignore the reasons someone should want to draw Muhammad, but it's also egregiously anti-intellectual. "If people get mad at your speech, stop speaking," is really just idiotic for anybody to think, let alone somebody who wants to be president. I should add, though, that Trump is not the only person, let alone the only politician, who reacted that way to the Garland attack.

Another example is Trump's praise for the "strength" of the Chinese in responding to the Tiananmen Square protests, or his praise for various oppressive leaders. He's got a real authoritarian streak. He admires despots and dictators, people like Putin who "can get things done."

"Getting things done" is wonderful if you're in business and engaging with people on a voluntary basis. But we have to make a sharp distinction between that and "getting things done" when you're heading up a government that wields force. That's a whole different ballgame.

I think all of this goes deeper than just free speech. I don't think a guy like Trump views free speech as a separate phenomenon, because I don't think he has any understanding or appreciation for what freedom itself means. I should add that I think most candidates out there—Sanders and Hillary certainly, and I think to a large extent the others who have been in the race—are about as bad as Trump on this. We live in a time in which most candidates for office are essentially authoritarians, and in which, sadly, the only real question is over how much they want to use the power of government to control your life.

The only thing that I find really unique about Trump is that he wears his authoritarianism on his sleeve, and, importantly, that his supporters seem to like that about him. That's certainly unpleasant, but I think it tells us something about the direction in which this country is going. That doesn't mean we can't fight it by educating people and promoting better ideas, but it is something we should take very seriously.

PART 3

Free Speech vs. "The Public Interest"

So long as a concept such as "the public interest" (or the "social" or "national" or "international" interest) is regarded as a valid principle to guide legislation—lobbies and pressure groups will necessarily continue to exist. Since there is no such entity as "the public," since the public is merely a number of individuals, the idea that "the public interest" supersedes private interests and rights, can have but one meaning: that the interests and rights of some individuals take precedence over the interests and rights of others.

—Ayn Rand, "The Pull Peddlers,"
Capitalism: The Unknown Ideal

Gutting the First Amendment

Steve Simpson July 17, 2014

Supporters of campaign finance laws have been apoplectic since the Supreme Court struck down a ban on corporate political ads in *Citizens United*. Having lost another big case this year in *McCutcheon v. FEC*, they now want to write their views directly into the Constitution.

Last week, the Senate Judiciary Committee approved a resolution calling for a constitutional amendment that would let government limit contributions to candidates and spending by and on behalf of them. The House will take up a similar proposal soon. To see where this amendment would lead if enacted, consider that the law in *Citizens United* prevented a group from distributing a film that criticized Hillary Clinton during her last presidential bid. During arguments in the case, the government's lawyer admitted that the law could apply to books as well.

At the core of this effort is the very dangerous view that freedom of speech isn't an inalienable individual right—a right to say what you want regardless of what others think—but a privilege that we exercise at the sufferance of "the public."

This is the prevailing view among many intellectuals and politicians today. Justice Breyer expressed it in dissent in *McCutcheon* joined by his three colleagues on the left. In his view, the First Amendment protects the "public's interest" in having its "collective speech matter." Sen. Patrick Leahy, D-VT, echoed this view when he complained in advance of a hearing on the proposed amendment that the Court is ignoring "the voices of all Americans" in order to "amplify the voices of billionaires and corporations."

This is a fashionable view—we need campaign finance laws to prevent rich and powerful "special interests" from drowning out the "the public." But being fashionable doesn't make it true.

After all, who is this "public" that allegedly isn't being heard? Does it include newspapers like the *New York Times* and the *Wall Street Journal*? Broadcasters like MSNBC and Fox News? Millions of bloggers and Facebook and Twitter users? Donors to hundreds of political and advocacy groups? Jaw-boning politicians?

This article was first published by *The American Spectator* on its website, Spectator.org.

The fact is, "the public" doesn't exist. Only individuals do. Terms like "the public" are never used to refer, literally, to every last person who lives in society. Instead, they are always used to justify one group of people using the force of law against others.

Consider how easy it is to define "the public" to mean groups whose ideas you favor. To Harry Reid and his allies, "the public" doesn't include the Koch brothers or Tea Party groups targeted by the IRS, but it does include unions, environmental groups and others who support unlimited government power.

Of course, the right sometimes does the same thing. But that's part of the point. The "public interest" can be used to justify any restriction on speech. No one ever admits that they want to silence others, so they invoke this magic concept to do that dirty work for them.

And make no mistake: silencing people is the point of campaign finance laws. Yale law professor Owen Fiss defended those laws in his 1996 book, *The Irony of Free Speech*, by saying that government may "have to silence the voices of some in order to hear the voices of others. Sometimes there is simply no other way."

Silencing the loudest voices is the only way to make sure "the public" gets heard over individuals. And it's always where campaign finance laws lead, because people easily find ways around them. Limit contributions to candidates, and people will spend money on their own ads. Prevent people from saying "vote for" or "vote against" and they will criticize candidates in other ways. That's why, in 2002, Congress passed McCain-Feingold, which banned groups from even mentioning candidates near an election. No restrictions on spending for speech can be successful unless *all* spending is restricted.

The solution to this creeping censorship is to defend free speech as a *right*, not a privilege. That right does not protect our "voices" or guarantee that we'll have "influence." It protects our *freedom* to speak. Whether we are loud enough, persistent enough, or articulate enough is up to us.

Amending the Constitution is a long shot, and today's effort will almost definitely fail. But tomorrow's may not. If you value free speech, now would be a good time to start making yourself heard.

McCutcheon v. FEC: Free Speech for Me or Free Speech for We?

Steve Simpson April 11, 2014

In recent years, the Supreme Court has issued a spate of generally good campaign finance decisions that move steadily closer to treating free speech the way it should be treated—as an individual right. Last week's decision in *McCutcheon v. FEC*, which struck down so-called aggregate contribution limits, is the latest example. As Chief Justice Roberts noted in his decision for the Court, aggregate limits, which cap the total amount that anyone can give to *all* candidates and committees during an election season, end up limiting the overall number of candidates one can support. "The government may no more restrict how many candidates or causes a donor may support than it may tell a newspaper how many candidates it may endorse."

This point isn't hard to grasp. If we have the right to speak out about politics and to support candidates, then surely a limit on the number of candidates we can support or the amounts we can spend on speech violate that right.

So why do so many people—including the four liberal justices on the Supreme Court—insist that campaign finance laws are constitutional? Under what theory can the laws be reconciled with the First Amendment?

The answer, as Justice Breyer illustrates in his dissent in *McCutcheon*, is the theory that the First Amendment's primary purpose is to protect "the public interest" over the individual's rights. In short, the theory is collectivism.

Here's how Justice Breyer describes his position: "the First Amendment advances not only the individual's right to engage in political speech, but also the public's interest in preserving a democratic order in which collective speech *matters*." (Emphasis in original) The "public's" "collective speech" matters, according to Breyer, when it "can and will influence elected representatives." That can't happen, however, when individuals are allowed to support too many politicians or spend too much money on speech, because "[w]here enough money calls the tune, the general public will not be heard."

But what is this "general public," what counts as its "collective speech," and what keeps it from being heard?

Keep in mind that there's no such thing as "the public," there are only individuals. Likewise, there's no such thing as "collective speech," there's only the speech—meaning the expressed views—of individuals.

So Justice Breyer's complaint boils down to this: Some individuals are spending lots of money to convince Americans to vote for the candidates they support, and other individuals—whom the Justice calls the "general public"—don't like it.

Justice Breyer claims that big spenders are preventing this aggrieved group from being heard. But how? Despite what you hear each election season, no one can use campaign money to "buy" votes. They use it to buy advertising and other campaign activities that attempt to persuade people to vote a certain way.

Contributing money to candidates or spending it on your own doesn't prevent anyone else from doing the same thing. Consider the many opportunities that every American has to try to influence the views of voters and politicians:

- They can contribute money directly to politicians.
- They can give to any of the many groups, like Americans for Prosperity and the Center for American Progress, that speak out about political issues.
- If they don't like the views of any existing groups, they can set up their own as many Tea Party sympathizers have.
- If they want to have a more direct effect on politicians, they can give money to a group that engages in direct lobbying.
- If they prefer to go it alone, they can use Facebook, set up a blog or some other sort of website, produce their own videos, or use Twitter as millions of people do.
- If they prefer something more traditional, they can do what many Americans did during the Obamacare debates and communicate directly with their representatives.
- If they don't like any of those options, they can write articles, op-eds and letters to the editor or just wait for one of the hundreds of other publications out there to express their views.

In a free society, you are guaranteed the right to speak, not the right to "be heard" or to have the influence that you would like to have—with politicians, voters, or anyone else. If you want to publish a newspaper or a blog, write a book or become a broadcaster, you have the right to do so. But no one guarantees that you will be articulate or successful or that you will be able to earn or raise the money to fund your effort. If we are going to complain that some people feel they are not being heard when others spend money on political speech, why not complain that they are also unable to compete with the *New York Times*, *Wall Street Journal*, Instapundit, or the Daily Beast?

Justice Breyer washes all of these distinctions and questions away in the great soupy mess of the "public interest." But who comprises this "public" and why doesn't it include people who want to spend a lot of money in elections? And who, by the way, is doing all the voting in these elections? The best way to influence a candidate is to vote him into or out of office. Don't the proponents of campaign finance laws trust voters to make up their own minds?

The answer is that a concept like the "public interest" is not meant to be understood or to refer to anything concrete. Its purpose in this context is to mask the fact that some people want to use the law to silence others—in this case, others who want to spend a lot of money during elections. No one could ever get away with silencing these people on the ground that their views were objectionable. So the would-be censors invoke the magic concept of the "public interest" and claim that those they want to silence are somehow excluded from the "public" and opposed to its "interests." How many times have you heard that the government must listen to "public opinion" rather than all those selfish, narrow, moneyed "special interests" who are trying to corrupt the system?

But there is no "public." There are only individuals, and their interests lie in being left free to think and speak as they wish. As Justice Roberts recognized, "[t]he whole point of the First Amendment" is to protect those individual rights. Protecting the "public interest" in "collective speech" flips that purpose on its head.

The writer Nat Hentoff has long used the phrase "free speech for me but not for thee" to describe a person who pretends to support free speech but in fact only supports it for himself. Justice Breyer's approach is a more sophisticated variation on this theme—and more dangerous given the many people who accept it. Call it, "free speech for *we* but not for thee."

An Interview with Steve Simpson on Campaign Finance Laws

Education News June 2, 2014

Michael F. Shaughnessy: *Steve, first of all, tell us about yourself—who you are, what you do, and how you got involved in this?*

Steve Simpson: I'm the director of Legal Studies at the Ayn Rand Institute in Irvine, California, where I write and speak about legal issues from the perspective of Ayn Rand's philosophy of Objectivism. I'm a lawyer by training and worked as a litigator for about twenty years before coming to ARI last October. Before that, I worked at the Institute for Justice in Arlington, Virginia, for twelve years as a constitutional lawyer specializing in freedom of speech and campaign finance, among other things. You can read more about ARI and me at ARI's website, AynRand.org.

MFS: *Now [about the recent Supreme Court case],* McCutcheon vs. FEC— *who is this McCutcheon and what is the FEC?*

SS: Shaun McCutcheon is an Alabama businessman who is active in Republican politics. "FEC" stands for "Federal Election Commission," which is the federal agency that oversees and enforces the campaign finance laws that apply to people running for federal office (as opposed to state offices, which are covered by state campaign finance laws).

Like many other activists, McCutcheon donates to the campaigns of politicians he supports. A couple years ago, he decided he wanted to donate to a lot of politicians, which federal campaign finance laws prohibit through what are known as "aggregate" contribution limits. Most people know that the campaign finance laws limit the amount anyone can give to a single politician. The current limit is $2,600. But before the *McCutcheon* case came along, few people knew that the law also limits the total amount you can give to all candidates and political committees. The laws are complicated, but the bottom line is that

---

This interview, which was conducted by Michael F. Shaughnessy, originally appeared on the website Education News (educationviews.org) under the title "Steve Simpson on *McCutcheon vs. FEC*."

you can't give more than about $123,000 in any two-year period to all candidates and political committees. The effect of the law is to limit the total number of candidates and committees to which you can contribute. McCutcheon wanted to give $1,776 to twelve more candidates than the law allowed. (The amount is not a coincidence; he was trying to make a point.) His question for the Supreme Court was simple: If I can give within the limits to, say, the first twenty candidates, why can't I give the same amount to the 21st?

The Supreme Court's response was fairly straightforward as well: The First Amendment protects the right to support candidates, so the limit is unconstitutional. Chief Justice Roberts, who wrote the decision for the Court, put the point this way: "The government may no more restrict how many candidates or causes a donor may support than it may tell a newspaper how many candidates it may endorse."

MFS: *I suspect most readers know the First Amendment—but give us a backdrop and overview, vis-à-vis this case.*

SS: It's always useful to remind people of the actual language of the First Amendment, so let's start there: "Congress shall make no law . . . abridging the freedom of speech, or of the press."

Campaign finance laws limit the amount of money anyone can donate to a candidate's campaign. Why would that abridge anyone's right to free speech? Consider that the purpose of a campaign is to convince people to vote for one candidate and against others. Campaigns do that ultimately by producing a lot of speech—typically in the form of advertisements, speeches, signs, TV appearances and the like—and to do that requires a lot of money. If you limit the money, you necessarily limit the speech.

You often hear the claim that "money isn't speech," which is literally true, but beside the point. It's also true that computers, printing presses, paper and pens are not speech, but preventing people from using them would be just as much a restriction on the right to speech as telling someone they can only devote a thousand words to expressing their views.

So the money-speech connection is simple logic. It's an application of the broader principle, which the Supreme Court has recognized for decades, that limiting people's ability to get their message out—by taxing newsprint, say, or telling them they cannot form groups and associations—restricts their right to free speech. So campaign finance laws limit free speech in two ways: by limiting what you can spend on speech and by limiting your ability to associate with and support candidates. In *McCutcheon*, as Justice Roberts pointed out, the law limited the number of candidates someone can support.

That's not the end of the analysis, though, because the Supreme Court has long held that the government can restrict the right to free speech for a "compelling" enough reason. This is a very troubling standard, because it requires the courts to try to balance the individual's right to free speech against the government's "interest" in limiting it, which is ultimately arbitrary. We can see how a standard like this works in practice by looking at the last forty years of campaign finance decisions, which have involved constant battles among the justices on the Court over whether the government has come up with a "compelling" enough reason for limiting speech in this area.

The primary argument for the laws is that large campaign contributions "corrupt" the government. Thankfully, in recent years the five conservative justices have viewed that argument with great skepticism. Their view, in essence, is that trying to influence politicians cannot be considered "corruption" in a nation with a representative form of government. Supporting a campaign is one way to try to ensure that your representatives actually represent your views.

In this case, Justice Roberts made an even simpler point: if making a contribution within the limits to one candidate isn't corrupting—which, by definition, it isn't—then giving the same amount to many different candidates can't be corrupting either.

MFS: *We often hear people claim that too much campaign spending is "bad for democracy." What do they mean and is there anything to that idea?*

SS: To answer this question, we need to be clear about what we mean by "democracy." It's important, because one reason a lot of people think campaign spending should be regulated is that they are confused about the nature of government in this country.

Some people use "democracy" to mean the same thing as freedom—that is, a nation in which the power of government is limited and individual rights are protected. Under that meaning, there can't be anything bad about spending money to express your opinions and support candidates. Freedom means you have the right to act according to your judgment in pursuing your goals, so long as you don't violate the rights of others. So you don't have the right to commit fraud or libel, for example, or to bribe officials, but if you don't do those things when you speak, you can say what you want and support candidates to your heart's content.

But that's not the real meaning of "democracy." It doesn't mean freedom, it means majority rule. And that's how many people use it today, including those who support campaign finance laws. Under this view, the majority's power is effectively unlimited and they get to have whatever laws they vote for.

Most people who think America is, or should be, a true democracy rather than a constitutionally limited republic support campaign finance laws on the grounds that no one should have a greater say in what government does than anyone else. If "the people" are supposed to rule, they say, then it is unfair for any one person to have more influence over what government does than anyone else. The principle of democracy is "one man, one vote," they point out. But allowing some to exert more influence than others effectively gives them more than one vote. That "corrupts" the system, they claim. If you accept this argument, then campaign finance laws make sense, because their purpose is to prevent anyone from having "too much" influence.

The point is this: Don't confuse freedom with democracy. Democracy means the majority gets to impose its views on everyone through the force of law. Freedom means the government is limited to protecting individual rights. Free speech flourishes under freedom because respecting people's rights means respecting their right to live according to their own judgment. In a democracy, though, free speech lasts only as long as the majority tolerates it. If we leave campaign finance laws on the books, that won't be long.

MFS: *Let's talk about people contributing money to a candidate (let's pick on Bill Gates) and then corporations contributing money and then unions contributing money—what are the good and bad perspectives on these three contributions?*

SS: Currently, only individuals can contribute to candidates. So Bill Gates and anyone else can give $2,600 to any one candidate and varying amounts to different committees depending on their type. Because of *McCutcheon*, there are no more aggregate limits. But corporations and unions are not allowed to contribute money directly to candidates or committees that contribute to candidates, although they can spend their own money on political ads and give money to groups that only spend money on ads. The Supreme Court's *Citizens United* decision freed them to do that.

In my view, corporations and unions should be able to contribute to candidates the way individuals do. Corporations and unions are associations—that is, they are groups of individuals organized for a particular purpose. Whether they decide to spend the money they've earned or pooled for political speech is up to the individuals in the group. So long as no one is forced to join and they follow whatever internal procedures they've agreed upon for making decisions, then they should be free to spend their money for whatever legal purpose they want.

You often hear the claim that if rich people, corporations, or unions are allowed to contribute freely to candidates or spend money on their own political speech, then they will be able to "buy" elections. But that's not at all true. The money either given to candidates for their campaigns or spent by individuals or groups goes to buy speech—meaning it seeks to persuade voters to vote one way or another—it does not buy anyone's votes. At the root of the complaints about money in elections is the view that voters cannot make up their own minds in the face of all that political advertising, which is nonsense. Whether you like the outcome of elections or not, the fact is that voters ultimately decide to vote the way they do. In a free society, each of us must have the right to try to convince people to adopt different ideas or to vote a different way. That's what all that money in elections seeks to do, and those who oppose it are ultimately opposing the idea that people are and should be free to make their own decisions.

None of this is to say that I agree with the decisions voters often make. The point is that they are able to make those decisions freely. If I don't agree, I have the right to convince them to choose differently. That's what the right to free speech protects—the right to try to persuade people to adopt different ideas. Money certainly helps to get our message out, but it does not win the debate. There are too many examples of big-spending candidates—Meg Whitman and Jon Corzine come to mind—who lost elections for that to be debatable anymore. Money is necessary for any candidate to be a contender, but to win, they need to convince the voters to vote for them.

MFS: *Now let's talk about payoffs and kickbacks—is there any proof that favors are given to large contributors? (If that were so, I would like to be ambassador to England. How much would it take?)*

SS: To my knowledge, there's no evidence that campaign contributions lead to political favors in any general or systematic sense. This has been researched and debated for decades, and supporters of campaign finance laws have never shown, as far as I know, that contributions lead to what's known as "quid pro quo" corruption—that is, contributions for special favors.

But those who think contributions lead to special favors for contributors aren't crazy, so it's worth examining the issue in more detail. Let's ask a different question: Why do people want to influence elections and politicians?

The answer is that government influences people. Government limits our freedom to produce, to earn money, to run businesses and to live our lives in myriad ways. Government controls so much of what we do today that it would be crazy not to try to influence it to try to preserve our freedom—by, for example, trying to influence elections and politicians.

Consider the businessman who faces a growing regulatory burden. The difference between two types of regulation can mean billions in revenue and sometimes the difference between staying in business and bankruptcy. Is he supposed to sit idly by and refuse to try to influence how those regulations are written or whether they are passed?

Or consider the taxpayer who sees politicians clamoring for more and more of his hard-earned income. Is he supposed to stay out of politics for fear of receiving "favors" in the form of lower taxes in exchange for his campaign contributions?

The problem, in short, is not that there is too much money in politics, it's that politics controls too much money, property, business, and personal freedom. Eliminate government's power to hand out benefits and burdens and you eliminate the incentive to try to influence it. I believe in a free society in which government has one essential purpose: protecting rights. That means preventing people from using force against each other—for example, by preventing crime and protecting people's rights to life, liberty, property, and the pursuit of happiness. If that were all government did, it wouldn't be able to redistribute income, hand out corporate welfare, or impose anti-competitive regulations on business, so there would be no point in trying to influence it the way people do today.

Obviously, this is a radical approach to government that Americans are not going to adopt anytime soon. But if we don't understand why people try to influence government, we will end up focusing on a symptom while ignoring the cause, and we will end up restricting free speech in the process.

The cause of all the efforts to influence government—whether it comes in the form of campaign contributions, lobbying, or something else—is our lack of any principled limits on government power. The real limit on what government does today is majority will.

Each election season, candidates practically fall all over themselves inviting voters to vote for them in exchange for all sorts of benefits, whether it is welfare for the poor, welfare for corporations, subsidies for this or that preferred business, bailouts for certain businesses, bailouts for foreclosed homeowners, or protectionist laws. The list goes on and on.

How can we say that it is proper for politicians to offer all of these benefits and burdens in exchange for votes, but the moment any pressure group seeks the same benefits in exchange for campaign contributions, that is somehow corrupt?

This isn't to defend all of this behavior. All of it is regrettable, because it is a tremendous waste of effort, time, and money, but much of it is necessary and defensible. I take the same approach to judging efforts to influence politics through lobbying and campaigning that I take to free speech: it all has to be legal, but that doesn't make it ethical. Just as you have the legal right to advocate stupid, destructive, and crazy ideas, you also have the legal right to try to convince politicians to redistribute income or pass protectionist laws, but sensible people should criticize you for that. But there's nothing at all wrong with trying to influence politics in order to lower taxes and spending, decrease regulations, and promote freedom.

People use the term "cronyism" a lot today, but they typically don't distinguish between ethical efforts to influence government and unethical ones. That's unjust, so let's try to set the record straight. Cronyism, which is obviously a negative term, should only be used to refer to those who are trying to convince government to use the power of law—which ultimately means force—to achieve something they could never do without government. They can't take the income of others or ruin someone else's business directly, so they try to convince their "cronies" in government to do it for them. Ethical influence essentially amounts to a form of self-defense against the increasing restrictions on freedom that government imposes. It's a businessman trying to convince politicians not to regulate his business or a taxpayer urging them not to tax away even more of his income or an advocacy group urging government to change these destructive policies across the board.

Many of the people who are widely criticized for allegedly "corrupting" politics today—the Koch brothers come to mind—are trying to influence government in a positive direction. They are actually opposing the political system that leads to cronyism, and I applaud them for it.

MFS: *A bit of history—what has been going on in terms of past Supreme Court decisions?*

SS: Here's the thumbnail sketch of the last four decades of campaign finance law.

The modern federal law, the Federal Election Campaign Act, was passed in the early 1970s. It limited both the amounts you could give to candidates and the amounts you or candidates could spend to get elected. In 1976 the Supreme Court struck down spending limits as a direct limit on speech, but it upheld contribution limits as a minor restriction that was necessary to help eliminate "corruption."

The Court did not define "corruption" carefully, however, so for the next three decades the Supreme Court and the lower courts were at the center of a struggle to define the term broadly, and thus allow more regulation of campaign financing, or narrowly and allow less. If you think "corruption" means bribery—that is, paying an official to abuse his power—then the campaign finance laws are superfluous, because we already have bribery laws on the books. If you define corruption broadly to mean anyone who influences a candidate or an election "too much"—which is how the supporters of campaign finance laws tend to define it—then the laws will expand to restrict more and more political spending and thus more and more speech.

To understand why the laws expand under a broad definition of corruption, consider how easy it is to try to influence elections or candidates despite the campaign finance laws. If the law limits the amount you can give to a candidate, you just spend that money on your own by, for example, paying for your own ads supporting the candidate. If restricting influence—either influence over the voters or the candidates—is the goal, then you have to restrict those ads as well, along with anything a person might do to try to get a candidate elected.

The high-water mark for regulation came in 2003, when the Supreme Court upheld the Bipartisan Campaign Reform Act, otherwise known as McCain-Feingold, for its sponsors. The law imposes all sorts of regulations on candidates and political parties and prohibited certain groups from spending any money on ads that mentioned a candidate near an election. When John Roberts took the helm as Chief Justice, the Court became more sympathetic to free speech and began to limit the government's power in this area. The big case, of course, was *Citizens United* in 2010, which struck down the McCain-Feingold limits on corporate and union advertisements that support or oppose candidates. After that, the Court struck down a law that pertained to tax-payer-funded campaigns and then the aggregate limits in *McCutcheon.*

So, the recent trend is toward greater protections for free speech. But that could change if the composition of the Court changes.

MFS: *Now, are corporations that contribute money people or entities and what has the Supreme Court said in this regard?*

SS: You often hear that corporations are not "people." Like the "money is not speech" argument, this one is technically true, but irrelevant. Yes, corporations are not "people"; they are groups of people. If we take the right of association seriously, corporations and any other groups must have the same speech rights as individuals.

And that is, in essence, what the Supreme Court held in *Citizens United.* The Court has held for over fifty years that the First Amendment protects not only the individual's right to speak, but his right to join with others to make his efforts to speak more effective. There is no good reason to treat corporations any differently than any other group.

MFS: *What have I neglected to ask?*

SS: I think we've covered the issue pretty thoroughly. Thanks!

About the Contributors

Steve Simpson

Steve Simpson has been defending freedom of speech for more than fifteen years, first as a senior attorney at the Institute for Justice, where he litigated constitutional cases in courts throughout the nation, and now as the director of Legal Studies at the Ayn Rand Institute, where he writes and speaks on a wide variety of legal and philosophical issues.

As a lawyer, Steve was involved in many precedent-setting free speech cases. He was the lead litigator in *SpeechNow.org v. FEC*, the case that created Super PACs, and co-counsel in *Arizona Freedom Club PAC v. Bennett*, IJ's successful U.S. Supreme Court challenge to an Arizona law that used tax revenues to fund political campaigns. Steve was also on the legal teams in *Swedenburg v. Kelly*, IJ's successful challenge in the U.S. Supreme Court to New York's ban on the shipping of wine across state lines, and in the landmark eminent domain case, *Kelo v. City of New London*.

Steve has spoken and written widely on constitutional issues, including freedom of speech, campaign finance law, property rights and economic liberty. He has testified in Congress and appeared on many television and radio programs, such as PBS *NewsHour* and *Stossel*. His writings have appeared in many publications, from the *Wall Street Journal* to the *Washington Post* to *Slate* and many others. Steve earned his law degree from New York Law School in 1994, where he was managing editor of the law review. He went on to clerk for a federal district court judge and work in private practice at the international law firm Shearman & Sterling before moving into constitutional law in 2001. He is a member of the bars of New York, New Jersey, and the District of Columbia. In 2014, Steve was a Lincoln Fellow at the Claremont Institute.

Find him on Twitter: @ssfreespeech.

Onkar Ghate

Onkar Ghate is the Chief Content Officer and a senior fellow at the Ayn Rand Institute. He is the Institute's resident expert on Objectivism and serves as its senior trainer and editor. For more than a decade, he has taught philosophy at the Institute's Objectivist Academic Center.

Ghate is a contributing author to a number of books on Rand's fiction and philosophy, including *Essays on Ayn Rand's "The Fountainhead"*;

Essays on Ayn Rand's "Atlas Shrugged"; *Why Businessmen Need Philosophy: The Capitalist's Guide to the Ideas Behind Ayn Rand's "Atlas Shrugged"*; *Concepts and Their Role in Knowledge: Reflections on Objectivist Epistemology*; and *A Companion to Ayn Rand* (Blackwell Companions to Philosophy).

His op-eds have appeared in venues across the ideological spectrum, from *Huffington Post* to CNN.com to FoxNews.com and Businessweek. com. He's been interviewed on national and international radio, including NPR and BBC Radio, and has appeared as a television guest on CNBC, KCET, Fox News Channel and the CBS *Evening News*.

A Canadian citizen, Onkar studied economics and philosophy as an undergraduate student at the University of Toronto and worked in the financial industry prior to joining ARI in 2000. He received his doctorate in philosophy in 1998 from the University of Calgary.

Elan Journo

Elan Journo is a fellow and director of Policy Research at the Ayn Rand Institute. He writes and speaks for ARI, is a senior editor and teaches at the Objectivist Academic Center. He leads the Junior Fellows program in Policy Research and Legal Studies.

Elan specializes in the application of Rand's ethics of rational egoism to public policy issues. His research and writing focus on the intersection of moral ideas and American foreign policy. His 2009 book, *Winning the Unwinnable War: America's Self-Crippled Response to Islamic Totalitarianism*, analyzes post-9/11 U.S. foreign policy from the perspective of Rand's philosophy. His upcoming book examines American policy toward the Israeli/Palestinian conflict.

Elan's articles have appeared in *Foreign Policy, Claremont Review of Books, Journal of International Security Affairs, Middle East Quarterly*, and in many popular media outlets, including FoxNews.com, *Los Angeles Times, Chicago Sun-Times, The Federalist*, Australia's *Herald Sun* and Canada's *Globe and Mail*. He has been interviewed on Fox News Channel, PBS, NPR and hundreds of radio programs nationally and internationally. Journo briefs congressional staffers and speaks regularly at conferences and university campuses, including Stanford, Berkeley, UCLA, New York University, George Mason University and the U.S. Naval Academy.

Born in Israel, Elan grew up and was educated in the United Kingdom before moving to the United States. He holds a BA in philosophy from King's College, London, and an MA in diplomacy from SOAS, University of London.

Find him on Twitter: @elanjourno.

Leonard Peikoff

Leonard Peikoff has spent more than sixty years studying, teaching and applying the philosophy of Ayn Rand. Having been Rand's foremost student, he is today the world's preeminent expert on Objectivism.

A great admirer of *The Fountainhead,* he first met Rand in 1951, when he was, in his own words, "an ignorant, intelligent seventeen-year-old." He read *Atlas Shrugged* in manuscript and was invited "to ask the author all the questions I wished about her ideas." For thirty years, Rand was his mentor, editor and friend. "We talked philosophy late into the night on countless occasions," he recalls. "It was, for me, an invaluable education." On her death in 1982, Rand named Peikoff heir to her estate.

Born in Winnipeg, Canada, in 1933 (but now a U.S. citizen), Peikoff studied philosophy at New York University and taught at several colleges and universities between 1957 and 1973. For decades he lectured on Objectivism to worldwide audiences through live appearances and audio transcription of his courses. His 1976 course on Objectivism's entire theoretical structure earned Rand's endorsement (she also participated in some of the Q&A periods) and became the basis for his book *Objectivism: The Philosophy of Ayn Rand* (1991), the first systematic presentation of her philosophy.

Peikoff is also the author of *The Ominous Parallels: The End of Freedom in America* (1983); *The DIM Hypothesis: Why the Lights of the West Are Going Out* (2012); and *The Cause of Hitler's Germany* (2014, excerpted from *The Ominous Parallels*).

Asked once to name his life's greatest achievement, Peikoff said: "I mastered Objectivism and presented it to the world."

Christian Beenfeldt

Christian Beenfeldt was a guest writer for the Ayn Rand Institute and holds a D.Phil. in philosophy from Oxford University.

Acknowledgments

I want to thank Elan Journo for his encouragement, editing, and guidance throughout this project. Onkar Ghate also provided valuable editorial feedback on the entire book.

Special thanks go to Chris Locke, Rikki Nedelkow, Keith Lockitch, Richard Ralston, Simon Federman, Donna Montrezza, Lin Zinser and Lew Hendrickson for pulling together the resources to publish the book in record time. Amanda Maxham provided a great idea for the cover design.

Finally, I'd like to thank my wife, Deb, for her unfailing support and encouragement.

****

This book was made possible thanks to the many individuals, foundations, and corporations whose financial contributions fund the work of the Ayn Rand Institute.

Additional Resources

To explore the ideas presented in this book further, visit
ari.AynRand.org/freespeech.

Read

"Free Speech" in *The Ayn Rand Lexicon*

Ayn Rand: Freedom of Speech, published in *The Ayn Rand Column.*
This short article, published in the *Los Angeles Times* when Rand was a
regular columnist there, addresses the crucial importance of property rights to freedom of speech.

Ayn Rand: Have Gun, Will Nudge, published in *The Objectivist Newsletter.*
Ayn Rand argued throughout her career that intellectual freedom requires both political *and* economic freedom. She eloquently illustrates that principle in this essay, which focuses on the FCC's efforts in the early 1960s to pressure broadcasters to "improve" the quality of their programming.

Ayn Rand: The Establishing of an Establishment, published in *Philosophy: Who Needs It.*
The threat to free speech from censorship is clear, but what happens when government *encourages* certain ideas? Rand's answer is that it produces the same result as censorship. "[A]ny intrusion into the field of ideas, for or against anyone," she writes in this timely essay, "withers intellectual freedom and creates an official orthodoxy, a privileged elite." Today we can see an example of that "privileged elite" among scientists and foundations who scramble to produce "scholarship" that confirms the orthodox position on climate change. And we can see the ominous consequences in the calls to investigate and prosecute dissenters.

Ayn Rand: Fairness Doctrine for Education, published in *Philosophy: Who Needs It.*

"The most ominously crucial question now hanging over this country's future," Rand writes in this essay, is "what will our universities teach at our expense and without our consent? What ideas will be propagated or excluded?" We are seeing the answer today, and government involvement in education—which, Rand argues, can only produce intellectual staleness and conformity, is a crucial cause. This essay is an important companion piece to her essay "The Establishing of an Establishment."

Ayn Rand: To Dream the Noncommercial Dream, published in *The Voice of Reason.*

Another powerful essay on what happens when government finances intellectual pursuits, this piece focuses on government funding of the arts. Rand illustrates that artists who wish to "free" themselves from the "shackles" of the free market and the need to earn their own living only end up binding the arts with the real shackles that only government can impose.

Ayn Rand: "Political" Crimes, published in *Return of the Primitive.*

In the 1970s, many argued that protesters who resorted to violence should be treated as "political dissenters" rather than the criminals they were. In this essay, Ayn Rand explains that the logical result of this idea will be to enshrine the notion of "political crimes" into law—for, if one can be excused of a crime because of the allegedly political nature of his act, one can be prosecuted on the same grounds. This essay is especially timely in light of the IRS investigations of Tea Party groups, constant calls for increased regulations of political speech, and criminal investigations of oil companies for challenging climate change orthodoxy.

Ayn Rand: The Cashing-In: The Student "Rebellion," published in *Return of the Primitive.*

The "free speech movement" which started at the University of California at Berkeley in the 1960s, is widely hailed today as a seminal and positive event in the history of free speech. Ayn Rand saw it as a grave *threat* to freedom. In this essay, she analyses the movement and its philosophical causes. Required reading for anyone who wants to understand what is happening on America's campuses today.

Ayn Rand: The Left: Old and New, published in *The Objectivist.*

In this essay, Rand points out that no matter what policies the American left has claimed to support through the 20th century—whether political equality, free speech, or a healthy environment—its dominant philosophy of mysticism, altruism, and collectivism will achieve the opposite. As proof, she traces the various incarnations of the left to show that it has steadily rejected all the ideals it claimed to support. At a time in which the left is rejecting free speech, this essay is particularly trenchant.

Ayn Rand: Racism, published in *The Objectivist Newsletter.*

Racism, according to Ayn Rand, is "the lowest, most crudely primitive form of collectivism." Holding that an individual's identity and character is defined by his genetic code or his skin color, racism, in her memorable words, "is a doctrine of, by, and for brutes." Yet the way to combat this vicious idea is not to practice a version of the same thing in reverse—by granting special privileges to certain groups based on race. It is to recognize the supreme importance of the individual. Affirmative action laws, Rand predicted in this 1963 essay, will inevitably lead to quotas and a race consciousness that can only exacerbate the problem. The hyper-race consciousness that surrounds us today confirms that Rand was right.

Ayn Rand: The Comprachicos, published in *Return of the Primitive.*

Why do today's college students seek safety from controversial ideas, demand trigger warnings and rage against Western ideals? Rand points to the dominant trend in education, which is not to teach young people how to think, but to disable their minds, leaving them unable to understand or face the challenges life holds. This tour de force critique of progressive education is essential reading for anyone who wants to understand young people today.

Watch

Unveiling the Danish Cartoons: A Discussion of Free Speech and World Reaction

The Danish cartoons depicting Muhammad sparked a worldwide controversy, the reaction to which raises urgent questions about free speech whose significance goes far beyond a set of drawings. This panel discussion featured Daniel Pipes of the Middle East Forum and Yaron Brook, executive director of the Ayn Rand Institute. Recorded on April 11, 2006, at the University of Southern California.

Freedom of Speech or Tyranny of Silence?

Following the attack on *Charlie Hebdo*, the intimidation of Sony Pictures over *The Interview*, and a growing climate of self-censorship, these panel discussions explore the future free speech.

The first, held in Boston on January 21, 2015, features Flemming Rose, foreign editor of the Danish newspaper *Jyllands-Posten* and author of *The Tyranny of Silence: How One Cartoon Ignited a Global Debate on the Future of Free Speech*; Onkar Ghate, senior fellow at the Ayn Rand Institute; Harvey Silverglate, co-founder and chairman of the Foundation for Individual Rights in Education; and *Boston Globe* syndicated columnist Jeff Jacoby. The moderator is Gregory Salmieri, a philosophy fellow at the Anthem Foundation for Objectivist Scholarship who teaches at Rutgers University.

The second, held the next day at Rutgers University and also moderated by Salmieri, features Flemming Rose, Onkar Ghate, and Robert Shibley, executive director of the Foundation for Individual Rights in Education. (Audio only)

Free Speech and the Battle for Western Culture

After the *Charlie Hebdo* attacks in Paris, many Western intellectuals questioned whether we are abusing our right to free speech. In this talk, Yaron Brook explains why it is imperative to defend this precious freedom. Recorded on January 21, 2015, in Irvine, California.

Free Speech Under Siege

After the attacks in Paris and Copenhagen, many began questioning whether the right to free speech includes the right to offend. In this talk, Steve Simpson, director of Legal Studies at ARI, explains why our "culture of sensitivity" reveals a troubling ignorance about the nature and value of free speech. Recorded on March 25, 2015, at Clemson University.

Charlie Hebdo, the West and the Need to Ridicule Religion

In this talk, Onkar Ghate argues that the *Charlie Hebdo* attacks revealed the price of the West's ongoing appeasement of religion. He urges Americans to criticize and even ridicule religion and offers advice on how to do that. Recorded on July 4, 2015, at Objectivist Summer Conference 2015 in Charlotte, North Carolina.

Attacks on Free Speech

In this talk for the Harvard Federalist Society, Steve Simpson discusses the link between the appeasing attitude toward Islamists among many Western intellectual and the culture of political correctness on campuses today. Recorded on September 30, 2015, at Harvard Law School in Cambridge, Massachusetts.

Morality of Freedom

This lecture by Onkar Ghate surveys the philosophical foundations of freedom as a moral and political ideal and analyzes the rise and decline of liberty in the West.

Listen

The Yaron Brook Show: What Happened to Free Speech?
In this episode, originally aired shortly after the *Charlie Hebdo* attacks, Yaron discusses the philosophical cause of the attacks and what they mean for the future of free speech in the West.

Freedom of Speech, "Islamophobia," and the Cartoons Crisis
ARI Fellow Elan Journo interviews Flemming Rose, the journalist at the center of the Danish cartoons crisis, about his book *The Tyranny of Silence: How One Cartoon Ignited a Global Debate on the Future of Free Speech.*

The Yaron Brook Show: Freedom of Speech and the Muhammad Cartoons
In this special episode, guest host Onkar Ghate analyzes the appeasing, victim-blaming attitude among many intellectuals toward the Islamist attack on a cartoon contest in Garland, Texas.

The Yaron Brook Show: The Climate Change Inquisition
In this episode, guest host Steve Simpson discusses the investigations by state attorneys general of Exxon Mobil and the Competitive Enterprise Institute for allegedly committing fraud in connection with their opposition to climate change orthodoxy. Guests include Sam Kazman, general counsel of CEI, Alex Epstein, author of *The Moral Case for Fossil Fuels*, and Walter Olson, senior fellow at the Cato Institute.

Ayn Rand: Censorship: Local and Express
In this 1973 talk, Rand analyzes the ideas that led to the Supreme Court's decisions in five "obscenity" cases and warns that those decisions "establish[ed] the legal and intellectual base of censorship" in America.

Ayn Rand: The Student "Rebellion" at Columbia University
In this radio program, Rand examines the 1968 student "rebellion" at Columbia University and the courageous opposition to it by a student group called the "Committee for Defense of Property Rights."

Ayn Rand: The Press in a Free Society
This recording combines two radio interviews in which Ayn Rand responds to questions from students about the role of the press in a free society.

Ayn Rand: Faith and Force: The Destroyers of the Modern World

So long as men accept faith over reason, Rand argues in this talk, they will eventually embrace force as the means of achieving their goals. This talk (and the essay from which it was derived) is crucial for understanding both the religious and secular mystics who oppose free speech today.

Ayn Rand: Issues in Education

In this 1964 radio program, Rand addresses the state of education in America, why students are fleeing from reason, and how to educate them properly.

About the Ayn Rand Institute

The Ayn Rand Institute believes that your own happiness is the moral purpose of your life, that productive achievement is your noblest activity and that reason is your only absolute. ARI challenges people to rethink their convictions from the ground up and to call into question the philosophical ideas and moral ideals that dominate the world today. By increasing awareness of Ayn Rand and understanding of her revolutionary ideas, ARI continues to make significant strides toward the ambitious goal of changing the culture.

Made in the USA
San Bernardino, CA
30 June 2016